A Thousand Pieces

A Story of Mercy,

A Thousand Pieces
by S. J. Buxton

© Forrest Press
San Bernardino, CA

ISBN 0-9712410-0-7
Library of Congress number 2001093087

**Publisher's Cataloging-in-Publication
(Provided by Quality Books, Inc.)**

Buxton, S.J.
    "A thousand pieces": a story of mercy, of courage,
of love / S.J. Buxton. -- 1st ed.
    p. cm.

    1. Buxton, Jerry--Health. 2. Traffic accident
victims--California--Rehabilitation--Religious aspects--
Christianity. 3. Traffic accident victims--California--
Family relationships. 4. Spiritual biography.
I. Title

RA772.T7D89 2001   617.1'028'09794
                          QBI01-700766

All Scripture quotations in this book are from the King James version of the Bible.

Printed in the United States of America
First publication 3000 October 2001

Printing and Design services: 7Dcreative.com

For additional copies contact:
Forrest Press
724 W. 26th St., San Bernardino, CA 92405
(909) 882-6999
www.forrestpressusa.com

Price $11.95

To Jerry, who lived it

Foreword

A Thousand Pieces is a powerful, emotional, faith-building story of one man's struggle for life. It is the moving account of the trial of a family's faith as they grapple with the enormity of his injuries and the intensity of his suffering. This is, also, a tribute to the countless family, friends, and total strangers who participated in the healing and recovery of Jerry Buxton.

You will find yourself moved with compassion and rejoicing with this family as they witness the triumph of the human spirit and the unmistakable healing power of God. The book is written in such a manner that you will feel personally acquainted with Jerry, his wife, and family.

I will confess that I cried, again, when I relived Jerry's accident as it was retold in this book. Even today, each time I witness him swing a golf club I am reminded, again, of the miracle working power of God. I am in full agreement with the medical staff that cared for Jerry—divine intervention sustained his life.

Read it and enjoy it.

> Jerry's very best friend,
> Berl Stevenson
> Pastor
> New Life Center
> El Cajon, California

Acknowledgements

I will begin with the Lord Jesus, who is the center of this book, and who absolutely is the author. He provided it all: the miraculous recovery, then the ability and the wherewithal to write and publish the story.

Lorraine Heter must not be overlooked, for without her, it is possible there would have been no story.

My family has made tremendous contributions, beginning with Jerry himself, who lived out the story, and who has subsequently suffered through my writing about it. Each of my children is an inspiration to me, and has been constant encouragement throughout this project. I especially thank Rebecca who has been so willing to read the manuscript and to suggest improvement. She also has worked closely with me in setting up marketing and distribution plans.

None of our family will ever neglect to thank both the administration and the medical staff of St. John's Regional Medical Center for their part in this story. I am especially grateful to Dr. Judy and Dr. Yu who arranged for Jerry and me to read his medical records, and who helped us to understand them. I feel a distinct gratitude for Dr. Yu who took the time to write for this book.

My special thanks go to those who read the manuscript, and then were kind enough to write material to be included in the publication: Berl Stevenson, Donald O'Keefe, Larry Alred, Charles Grisham, Ed Cantu, and Nathaniel Wilson.

I thank Holly for her medical insight.

Ed Cantu thoroughly critiqued the manuscript and made timely and pertinent suggestions. I would have been totally lost without Rebecca Juarez who read repeated drafts of the book, and who became my personal grammar and punctuation guru.

I am grateful to Tara Bollmann and Matt Jones who came to my rescue during the very end of this project. They pointed me in the right direction as far as graphic design and printing were concerned.

Thank you—all of you.

Preface

Many people have said this book should be written; I agreed with them and knew I should be the one to write it, given my proclivity for such a project, and being so closely involved with its experiences and its characters. The story that is mine to tell, despite its tragic core, is one of heroic adventure, one not planned, not calculated, certainly one whose revisiting would not be desired, yet one whose edges hint at transcendent glow and whose cusp is aglitter with wondrous glory. It is a story ripe with golden goodness, bursting with the philosophy of excellence and of the higher aspect of man. It is high drama, a theatre of faith, a God-lifting.

The account of my husband's severe accident, his virtual death, yet his subsequent recovery is so profound and moving as to have wide benefit to society at large. At opposite poles from one of negative and immoral bent, the story is one of the goodness of mankind, of faith, and of courage.

A chunk of stone struck by an artist may appear damaged and degraded. With swift chisel he wields insult, marring the line, forcing a shadow, laying a plane. From side to side he moves, his knowing eye eternally judging. Finally the piece is finished, glowing its lustrous beauty. The artist stands aside; the masses pass before it and weep. Wrenched from the quarry heap has emerged a masterpiece: a statement, a message, a sermon.

The Incident

.... I am in a great strait: let us fall now into the hand of the
Lord, for His mercies are great."

II Samuel 24:14

1

Screaming brakes slashed the afternoon air. Tortured wheels whined at high pitch digging into the hot pavement as the truck careened crazily, strewing debris in its path. It roared by me, mere inches from my face. A flare of red, its tires exploded as it leaped the high curb, then smashed into the freeway fence. I gasped as graveled dirt and spent car parts funneled a tornado that circled me. My mind was a broiling torrent, and I turned my head toward the street and to the lone car that sat there. Nothing moved, and I could see no one. Frantic, I yelled into the void. "Where is my husband?" There was no answer.

It was near 5:00 o'clock, August 6, a Saturday evening in 1994—the location was Oxnard, California. Jerry and I were on our way home, having spent the previous week at a church camp in Santa Maria. We had left our motor home there, would be at our own church for the Sunday services, then would return to Santa Maria on Monday, where Jerry would help with the district youth camp.

Our vehicle to get us to Rialto and back to camp was a 1974 Toyota Landcruiser. I remember the day we found it on a small car lot in Missouri, and that instantly Jerry wanted it. He and the other guys kicked the tires and peered at the motor and we ladies grinned.

The necessary money came forth, and it was ours. The jump seats were missing, so we drove to the previous owner's farm to get them, and when we got there, they directed us to the barn. "Just climb in and look around for the things," they said.

At home in California, Jerry dinked around with his treasure, had it painted, and put new covers on the seats. He coddled it, driving it on errands around town, and when we took motor home trips, it followed smartly behind us.

That Saturday, I had ridden with my friend Lil from Santa Maria as far as Rincon, a beach recreation area, meeting other friends for lunch. There, I rendezvoused with Jerry. Upon arriving at Rincon, he had begun poking around under the hood of his car, reporting that he was having trouble with it: "I don't know what the matter is. It just is not running right." He was able to start the engine though, and after eating sandwiches, we said good-bye to our friends and headed south on Highway 101.

At a nearby lake, *Frank and Oscar carried their fishing gear from the boat, along with coolers and the left over six packs, transferring them to their red truck. They had gotten up at 2:00 that morning, had fished all day, and they were now exhausted. Oscar climbed into the back, bedded himself beneath the truck cover, and soundly fell asleep while Frank took the wheel. He was very tired. He was legally drunk. He headed south toward Highway 1.

*Not their actual names

As we neared Oxnard, our car began cutting out again, and Jerry decided to leave Highway 101 and head into town to get it repaired. We took the Highway 1 exit that is also called Oxnard Blvd, and at that moment the car acted as though it would stall. Jerry pulled to the shoulder, and when he had raised the hood and jiggled wires again, he was able to restart it. We traveled about a quarter of a mile when it began to misfire once more. We ran down a hill, under a rail overpass, then starting up the other side the engine faltered and died. Jerry pulled to the side of the road, as far as possible, the car resting against a high curb.

Moderately heavy traffic moved at 50-60 miles an hour making its way over the four-lane thoroughfare. It was daylight, and the road was dry. "It is dangerous here," Jerry calmly spoke to me as he sat behind the wheel. "You need to get out of the car." I did so, moving 15 or 20 feet away while looking around for a place to get help. Nearby, I saw various businesses. Behind me was a residential area. Across the street was a Levitz furniture store.

Lorraine Heter was a public school teacher who had watched her father die from a heart attack when she was thirteen years old. Feeling helpless, she had resolved to be prepared should a similar situation arise. She had taken numerous CPR classes, the most recent of which had dealt with the handling of an accident victim who may have sustained spinal cord injuries. In the Heter home, a few days before this one, two dining room chairs had inexplicably broken. On this Saturday, she, her husband, and their two daughters headed north from Disneyland, drove through Oxnard, and pulled into a furniture parking lot where they would replace the chairs. It was hot; Lorraine got the girls out of the car and prepared to give them a drink of water.

On the street, Jerry raised the hood, then walked to the driver's side of the Landcruiser. Investigators' reconstruction of the scene placed him standing just inside the open door. I stood on the side of the street, my back turned away from the car.

The red Nissan truck roared down Oxnard Blvd. with Frank fighting sleep and fatigue, his mind blurred from alcohol and methamphetamine. Later, he would say he did not see the Landcruiser.

Suddenly the right side of his truck rammed into the Landcruiser's bumper, a three-inch steel pipe that bent inward now, the truck slicing into the metal as it slid along the car, trailing its scarlet paint. It slammed into Jerry then, a blow that lifted him from the pavement and jammed both knees into the car door, leaving concave rounds. He was catapulted over the door.

Tires exploding, piercing peals of ripping metal, hot wheels askew, and shattering glass melded into 20th century sound of automobile accident. The sound entered my ears, in milliseconds reached my brain, and registered: our car has been hit. Somewhere in that miniscule period, the red Nissan flew by me and came crashing to a stop at the freeway fence. I looked toward the Landcruiser, seeing no one. My mind ricocheted wildly. Perhaps he is behind it, and I cannot see him. I willed it to be so. My eyes jerked back and forth, frantically searching. I saw no one and have recollection only of silence. Nothing. No one moved. The Landcruiser sat alone on Oxnard Blvd. "Where is my husband?" I screamed.

Turning my body then, I looked south on Oxnard Blvd, and there, 86 feet in front of the car, lay a mound of body. It cannot be…can't be… my mind protested. Everything seemed to be in slow motion—a fog. I ran toward him, and before I could reach him, I saw a lady kneel down beside Jerry and prepare to move him. "Don't touch him," I screamed at her. Lorraine Heter raised her face to look at me. "Ma'am, he is not breathing, and he has no pulse."

Jerry's body was twisted 180 degrees, so that his buttocks lay on the black pavement, as did his face. His forehead had dug into the asphalt, reddening it now, and chunks of wood and gravel were embedded in his flesh. His eyes were closed. Carefully, Lorraine maneuvered him, still observing his lack of breath. Explicitly recalling her extensive training and preparation for this very moment, Lorraine pressed on his chest. It gave under her hand, the structure destroyed. Trembling, she pressed again, and far beneath his splintered ribs, the bruised heart roused, and began anew its beat of life. With a shudder, he drew in a faltering breath.

His head was a torrent of blood. "I'll get something for it from the car," I spoke to Lorraine, and started that way. However, my feet were cement—heavy chunks stuck on the end of rubber legs. In my peripheral vision, I saw a young man throw his head forward extending his arms to pull his shirt over his head, and I turned back toward Jerry.

"Here, take this," he said, handing his shirt to Lorraine.

Then Frank turned toward me, and with eyes directed to the ground he spoke: "I am sorry, Lady." I cannot recall my response.

A crowd had formed, and in the distance, I heard a siren. Helpless, I knelt beside him, touching Jerry's torn body, detached, alone with him. A lady bent over and told me which hospital to choose, and I remember saying that I was sure the best one would be selected. The crowd parted as the ambulance halted, the pitch of its siren fell then jerked to a stop. The paramedics ran with their equipment. The leader knelt down, checked him, then looked up and said to his colleagues, "Let's go." They immobilized him with full C-spine bracing, then a board was slid beneath him. They used sandbags to wedge him tightly, and then completed the fastening with wide bands of tape drawn over his inert body. One of the attendants bent forwards and placed a plastic mask over Jerry's face. A black hose and a football shaped bag trailed from the mask. The attendant began squeezing the bag, forcing oxygen into Jerry's tattered lungs.

I bent over him as they pushed him through the ambulance doors. "Hang on, Jerry. You're going to make it." Perhaps I imagined it, but I thought his eyes fluttered slightly.

I could not ride with him, a policeman told me, and so I stood and watched as the revolving lights began their flash, the sirens came to full pitch, and the ambulance pulled into the street. Some 90 feet away, the Landcruiser sat jammed against the curb. I looked over at the red truck and saw Frank and Oscar busily moving things around. Later, I saw a policeman arrange beer cans on the tailgate, then take out a camera and snap pictures of the stack.

By this time, I was frantic to get to the hospital. "How will I get there?" I pled with an officer.

"I will take you as soon as I finish the investigation."

"No, I must go now," I insisted.

Wearing shorts, and with a mustached face, a tall man stepped toward me. "I will take you."

I stared at this stranger, not speaking, and the policeman addressed me: "This man will take you."

"Do you know him?"

"No, but he seems to be a nice man."

The man pulled out his wallet. "Here is my identification. Rick Manzer."

What should I do? I felt desperate to get to the hospital, this man appeared respectable, but then again so do ax murderers, my mind warned me. Within moments, though, I decided, and looking directly into the man's dark eyes spoke: "Thank you. Let me first go to the car and get my calendar. It has telephone numbers that I will need."

He took my hand and led me around the corner. I was terrified. His vehicle was a large van, and when he opened the door to hand me in, I saw that both his seat and mine were covered with ropes. Terror clamped me, my breath coming in jerks, and as he walked to the driver's side, I formed a plan. Moving my hand forward, I firmly placed it on the door handle and resolved that at the first inkling of anything amiss I would press on the handle and jump. I did not fasten my seat belt. No matter where we were, how heavy the traffic, how fast we moved, I would jump.

We turned and headed down Oxnard Blvd. "They are taking him to St. John's," Rick told me, "and it is close by." I sat in silence, entombed in a world that in fifteen minutes had splintered into a thousand pieces. Within minutes, we pulled into the hospital parking lot. Rick opened my door, took my hand, and led me in.

2

It was 4:57 when Gold Coast Ambulance Service received notification of the automobile accident on Oxnard Blvd; one minute later the ambulance was in route and two minutes later was on the scene. The paramedics worked with Jerry in the street for several minutes, and now, at 5:09, were in the ambulance with him, heading for St. John's Regional Medical Center. They could barely keep him alive, mechanically assisting his breathing by "bagging" him. They were unable to get a blood pressure reading at all. An IV needle was inserted into one of his arms. He responded neither to verbal commands, nor to painful stimuli, although when a light was shinned into his eyes, his pupils reacted equally, a positive sign. The attendants continued the delivery of oxygen that had been started in the street. His skin was noted to be pale, moist, and cool to the touch. They communicated with the hospital saying they were underway and briefly describing the critical condition of their patient. "Estimated time of arrival: 5:13."

It is fair to call a hospital emergency room a battlefield, for death lurks there, slinking through every sweep of the clock hand and over every turn of the calendar page. Death pursues life, sneering, grasping, and often overtaking it. The hospital, however, is vigilant, resisting death's advances, mounting a guard, prepared and waiting.

They were prepared for Gerald Buxton, expecting him, having in readiness their large trauma unit, fully staffed and expertly equipped. At 5:13, he was handed off, the responsibility of the flying gurney and its occupant transferred from Gold Coast to St. John's. With courage, and no doubt a fair amount of trepidation, the emergency room staff received him, launching once more an all out and fierce assault against death.

3

Rick Manzer was an angel, disguised as a man who wore cotton shorts and whose upper lip supported a thick, black mustache. Still holding my hand, he led me up to St. John's Regional Medical Center, through the emergency room door, and to the admissions window. Rick told the clerk I was the wife of the man who had been brought in by ambulance; she smiled at me, and spoke gently. "There is some paper work to do." She asked questions, and we slid papers back and forth, one being our medical card. That finished, she said a doctor would speak to me as soon as possible. I needed to make phone calls, and in response to my question she directed me to a booth in the corner of the room. There were few people there, and though no one watched, a TV blared, while several children played with their toys. As we prepared to make calls, a social worker came over and directed us to a private room with a telephone.

"Your husband is critically injured, and a doctor will be out to talk with you as soon as he can," she said. "Try to make yourself comfortable in this room. If there is anything else we can do for you, please let us know."

Rick dropped coins in a machine, set a drink in front of me, and asked, "Whom do you need to call? I will help you." He touched my arm and patted me gently. In my address list, I found the numbers I needed. Rick actually did the dialing, handing me the receiver once he had a person on the line. Knowing my four children were hours away, and needing someone to be with me immediately, the first number we called was the home of Kenneth Fields, a pastor in Oxnard. I spoke with his wife, Joyce, telling her what had happened, and she promised to come to the hospital immediately. "What does she look like?" spoke the black-haired angel. "I will watch the door and bring her to you."

Michael, our second-born son who lives in Lake Havasu, Arizona was the first child I reached. Though I tried to be delicate with my words, the story was nothing but grim, and as I related the few details I knew, he moaned, and protested, "No, Mom, no. Not Dad." For a few seconds, while he struggled to gain his composure, and as his mind grappled with the significance of the words he had just heard, a leaden silence of horror sagged between us. Then I heard him speak loudly to someone in the office. "My dad has been in a terrible accident." Then he said to me, "Mom, hold yourself together. I love you, and Melina and I will be there as quickly as we can." We discussed the possibility of them flying instead of driving, but because of distances from major airports, he decided it was best to drive. It would be sometime the next morning before he could get to the hospital. He asked about the other children, and when I told him he was the first I had reached, he offered to call Andrew and Rebecca to let them know. I would call Steve.

Steve is our eldest, and I knew he was still at the Santa Maria fairgrounds, where the youth camp was to start that night. He had no cell phone, and I did not have a number for the fairgrounds. Rick called information, but the only number we could get proved to be a recording. I had a list of ministers, and we tried calling Rick Keyes, who is a pastor in Santa Maria. There was no answer at his home, and I concluded that he was probably at the youth camp also. After trying everything we could think of, finally Rick brilliantly said, "I will call the Santa Maria Police Department." When he reached the watch officer and explained the situation, he was assured that one of their team would be dispatched immediately to locate Steve.

Rick spotted Joyce Fields as she entered the hospital, and when he brought her to me, she hugged me tightly. I believe I cried. It was such a relief to have my friend with me and she was a tremendous comfort. Yet my body still trembled, and my head roared with all that was going on. "I will stay right here with you. And I have reached my husband, who will be here shortly," she told me. We left the telephone room and sat in the emergency waiting room. Rick took my hand again, telling me he must leave, but that he would come back later. I looked into the black eyes of this stranger who had scooped me off the street, and thanked him, saying I would never forget what he had done. He had stayed with me over an hour.

Larry Alred is a pastor in Ventura, a town just a few miles from Oxnard. He and his wife are close friends of ours. Joyce Fields called him right after she arrived at the hospital, and within a few minutes he was there with us. He expressed his sorrow and his grave concern for Jerry.

Finally a doctor came[1], saying Jerry was critically injured, and giving little hope for his survival. "May I see him?" I asked. He hesitated, closely observing me, no doubt his long experience telling him that I must be distraught and emotionally vulnerable. He was right. I was a quivering mass of protoplasm awash on cruel sea, thundering storm having savagely wrenched me from land. I had been thrust into deep and frigid water, black and fierce. Yet, lay my life partner more battered than I, infinitely more, plunged deep into fearful and unknown abyss, his life now rapidly fading. Trembling, my mind rejected the thought of new assault; still, I knew I must be with him. "I will see my husband," again I said to the doctor. "I am strong, and I believe I can handle it," I spoke with quavering voice. "Take me to him."

---

[1] *I am not sure of the names of every doctor I spoke with, nor in what order. Medical charts record that Drs. Yu, Cardan, Rimoldi, Star, Kadin and Fineberg were involved with Jerry's care on that Saturday night.*

Larry Alred went with me. The doctor pushed a button, doors opened, and he led us to Jerry's cubicle. Glistening lights flared their white, hot glow. Machines sounded; his life indicators were green numbers over his head. Hanging bottles swayed, and lines and cords twisted. A respirator bellowed, giving him one breath, then another. Blue-and-white-frocked people surrounded his bed—doctors, nurses, and technicians—but they let us walk to him. His battered head was swathed in a white cloth, and he lay stone still, yet I was told that on some level he was conscious. I patted his poor arm, and he opened his glazed and bottomless eyes. He looked at me, and around the respirator tube jammed down his throat mouthed the terrifying words, "Help me."

Jerry lay in profoundly critical condition with massive, almost unimaginable injuries. I watched as a nurse adjusted his transfusion line. On a steel table coated with plum colored residue, lay empty plastic bags and rounded full ones. "Keep three units ahead," I heard someone say. Somewhere inside my husband a deadly hemorrhage gushed. They placed X-ray machines over him, studied laboratory reports, and moved him to other rooms then back again for tests that could not be done in the emergency room.

From time to time, as the medical staff diagnosed and charted his injuries, and as Jerry fought valiantly to live, they let me go into the emergency room and stand by his side. Once, as I stood a distance from his bed while they performed a procedure, a nurse, not knowing who I was, read from a new report and declared, "It would be easier to say what is not broken on this man, than what is." I sensed that someone signaled who I was, and she turned away and said no more. His chest had drastically expanded; blood and other fluids filled the cavity as his tissues began to swell.

"I can't breathe," he mouthed to a nurse. Dr. Kadin brought a sharp knife, and, cutting through skin and muscle, entered one of his lungs, where he inserted a drainage tube that was connected to a suction device. Fluids gushed, and his breathing eased.

Once in the waiting room, I saw two police officers enter, a young man walking between them. I recognized him to be Frank, and I was startled when I saw that his hands were shackled and drawn behind his back. Before this moment, I had not really considered the implication of the stacked beer cans I had seen on the tailgate of their truck. Now I thought of that scene, and wondered what it all meant. I considered, too, that Frank could possibly have some injuries.

Hours passed before Jerry's condition had been completely assessed and he was considered stable enough for surgery. A doctor came to say they would be moving him to surgery, directing us from the emergency waiting room to another down the hall. "We will keep you posted on his condition," he said. He would be in surgery for many hours, with several surgeons operating. Later we learned that his list of injuries was long. He had major head trauma with deep and severe lacerations on his forehead; multiple rib fractures; one punctured and collapsed lung; and a femur/hip fracture on the right side with a hematoma extending to his knee. His pelvis was fractured and splayed, and his clavicle was broken. He had no circulation in his lower extremities, his urinary bladder was ruptured, and a large pelvic hematoma had formed. He was bleeding profusely, receiving eight units of blood in the first 45 minutes he was in the emergency room. He was in shock, had a widened mediastinum, had multiple central lines placed, and he had been connected to a ventilator with nasotracheal intubation. A nasogastric tube had been placed in his stomach. He had multiple contusions and lacerations over his lower extremities bilaterally, his liver was lacerated, and his heart was bruised. His right tibia was fractured, and he had multiple ligamentous injuries of his left knee.

Incidents

Beginning well before that lightening moment of conception, each individual evolves as a series of incidents. These incidents form a silvery life thread that circles and twists in on itself—revealed design that becomes our very essence. An insult to the developing embryo may signal gnarled limb or sightless eye; thus, may strongly influence occupation, hobby, length or breadth of life, height, and circumference. Add a fall, certain parental instruction, emotional nurturing or deprivation, a teacher, or a lesson learned. The selection of car, choice of route, chance of time, to lunch or not to lunch—these incidents may seem inconsequential, yet their cumulative value marks and defines us.

God rules within these wide parameters, this space of chance. He is the one who spoke to nothing and the worlds blazed, who poured out the seas of seven, who threw stars to spangle midnight ink, who set wood ducks to pond, and who swam gold fishes in green waters. It was He who groomed Eden, then lovingly shaped Adam and Eve. This God, this very God, oversees His world, our world, orchestrates and directs it.

How so? you ask. Explain misfortune and accident then. Can it be that a loving God who controls everything and who sits supreme would allow the pain and suffering of an innocent child or tragedy to those very ones who claim to love Him and to serve Him—His own children? Can there truly be a God who is involved in the day to day affairs of men? How can one say God cares and is concerned and watching when good people are struck down and when guileless and helpless ones are twisted and warped? How can it be so?

An understanding of the nature of God is imperative, as is a fresh look at Eden. The central nature of God is absolute holiness and exacting righteousness. Sin will not be tolerated in His presence; indeed, it cannot be. Linked, though, to these attributes are mercy and grace and a love so intense that it caused this God of glory to cloak Himself in mortal flesh then to slip down to earth as a wide-eyed baby. He grew, ran the gamut of human suffering, then gave His hands to ringing hammer, to death, and to burial. Yet on the third day He rose, His power intact, His strength undiminished.

With arrogant stride, Lucifer had paraded in paradise, offering tantalizing fruit to Eve. In the cool of each evening, God walked with Adam and Eve, giving them instructions and specifying which fruit to avoid. Eve ignored God's words, freely ate of the forbidden fruit, then Adam ate also. The result was sin, judgment, and banishment from the garden. Thus, today have come grief and sorrow, incidents of horror and of distress. Life flows: a mutation here, pain, a fetus ripped from its nest, a twisting, plans gone awry. It is not God who ordered it so, nor does He sit each morning dictating a misshapen kidney, a faltering pancreas or an accident on Oxnard Blvd. Able to prevent it all? Yes. Bound by His own righteous nature? Yes. Thus, we live in a world designed by God, intended for perfection, but a fallen one. Days pass, incidents unfold; some are good, some bad, a negative force, and now a positive.

A decade ago, in His mercy, did He prepare Lorraine Heter to tend Jerry? Did He cause her sturdy chairs to break for no obvious reason so that she would pull into the Levitz furniture parking lot? Probably. Did He send Frank, drunk, down Oxnard Blvd. to strike down Jerry? Of course not. But, how do we know? How can we be sure? In all honesty and with strict accuracy, of course, we cannot say; there exist questions that may never be answered. Of this, though, I am convinced: all that happens to me has passed through the hand of God, and He alone determines—yes, this may happen, or no, it may not. At times, as we pass through trying and puzzling days, we come to the other side, look back and understand the reason; we see the lesson learned. However, at other times, we do not; we never understand, never know the sense.

The book of Hebrews offers insight into this subject, as it describes a number of God's faithful people. Much of the eleventh chapter deals with righteousness, the overcoming of obstacles, miraculous deliverances, the hands-on blessing of patriarchs, and the snatching of prey from roaring beast. Riveting, victorious accounts are reviewed. Note that toward the chapter's end another aspect is recorded, the roll call shouting for others: the tortured, the mocked and scourged, the prisoner, the one sawn asunder, and the destitute—those seemingly defeated and cast down. Were they rejected of God, unloved, uncherished by Him? No, absolutely not. Was God not watching, not hearing, not seeing, and not feeling during the days of their trials? Despicable thoughts these, fashioned and flamed in the bowels of hell, then flung full-force into the minds and souls of such tormented people. It is obvious, though, that Paul, as he wrote those words to the Hebrews, had a clear understanding of absolute truth. For he finished this astonishing account with powerful words that define these peoples' ultimate end. The world is not even worthy of them, he said. "These all have obtained a good report…" (Hebrews 11) Each one was commended for his faith.

Whence and how comes a soul? Invisible and mysterious in beginning, God creates each one, giving it spirit and a body. Let it be emphasized that life is a continuum, incidents before our birth and throughout our lives influence our way and our ultimate decisions and destination. Genetics, the chance of birth, family culture, the locale of our living, exposure to danger, teaching, and societal forces combine to fashion the human being. Squarely, we must face our unique situation and our affected selves, doing so without flinching and without complaint; rather, with courage and fortitude. Using our gifts and resources, we are to deal with the inevitable hurt, for there also come joyous and happy times, bursting in on us as shot flames that sear a holiday night-sky. Our assignment: Put together the days of joy and the nights of sorrow in such a way that these incidents mark us as progressing, developing human beings, eyes set, gaze fixed on the glorious eternal good.

The Family

"Remember that you are an actor in a play, and the Playwright chooses the manner of it. ...Your business is to act the character that is given you and act it well; the choice of the cast is another's."

Epictetus

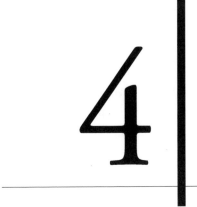

STEVE

At the Santa Maria Fairgrounds, the opening service of the senior youth camp was scheduled for Saturday evening. Throughout the day, young people and staff gathered, registering and settling into their designated dormitory rooms. Steve Buxton had spent the day helping to get things completely set up and organized for the several hundred teenagers that would be there by nightfall. There was a strangeness about his day, and he felt uneasy, to the extent that once he mentioned it to his wife, Dearrah, saying he felt concerned about something. At one point, he specifically mentioned his parents. "I hope they are all right." He was tense and felt a sense of fear.

Around 7:00 o'clock, Rick Keyes and Berl Stevenson met the policeman who came to the front gate of the Santa Maria Fairgrounds asking for Steve Buxton. Being a close family friend, Berl drove off in a golf-cart to find Steve. Not realizing anything serious had transpired, he began teasing him. "What's wrong, Steve? Forget to pay a ticket?"

After Steve had shown identification, the policeman asked him: "Do you know Gerald Buxton?"

"Yes, he is my father."

He handed Steve a piece of paper with a telephone number on it. "You need to call this number. Your father has been involved in a serious automobile accident."

They frantically drove to where Dearrah was, and then they dashed to a phone booth. By the time Steve finished his conversation with a nurse at the hospital a supporting wall of ministers had gathered. Steve could hardly speak as he hung up the phone. He turned first to Berl and told him the dreadful story, and then Berl recounted it to the rest of the group. Their immediate reaction was shocked unbelief. Quickly someone said, "Let's pray."

Steve's children, Chris and Joel, must be told; Harvey Cantrell, the district secretary went to get them from the auditorium. Then going to the microphone, he called the entire audience into a special time of prayer for Jerry's life.

Stunned, Steve and his family threw clothes together, and set out for the two-hour trip to Oxnard. The boys went with Paul Wilson and Sam White (ministerial friends of ours) in a truck, while Paul Price (the district superintendent) drove his car, in which Steve, Dearrah, Berl, and his wife, Lavelta, rode. A ghastly silence hung in the car, words stuck in tightened throats. Finally, they arrived at the hospital. Steve ran into the emergency room and found me sitting there, although I have no exact recollection of his arrival. I wore a wrinkled plaid jacket, and later he would describe me as appearing dazed.

REBECCA

She answered the phone herself when Michael called. "Rebecca, Mom and Dad have been involved in an accident, a bad one." She stood in the dining room, and as she heard the frightening words, she felt herself melting into the wall, slouching on it for support. "Dad has severe head injuries, and they don't know if he will live or not."

"Mom? What about Mom?"

"She is fine," he replied. Then he told his sister all the details he knew. "Mel and I are leaving shortly for Oxnard."

She hung up the phone, and immediately told her husband Greg. They snatched a few clothes, threw them in their car, and headed for the hospital. During the two-hour trip, she felt frantic to be with us, her now fragile mom and dad. She despised the distance and time that separated us. Though sitting beside her husband in the speeding car, she felt alone and desolate; her mind shattered into violent, disconnected thoughts, icy spears of dread and frustration.

Greg parked the car quickly at the hospital parking lot, and together they ran into the emergency room. "Where is my dad? Where is Mr. Buxton?" Rebecca asked at the desk. The clerk pointed down the highly polished tile floor, showing them the room where we waited. Rebecca ran to me and embraced me tightly. She wanted to see her dad immediately, but she could not for he still was in surgery. Turning to our friends who waited with me, she greeted them. We discussed all the known details, and then she left the room. For a long time she wandered through the halls, wanting to be alone, praying that God would spare her dad. "Please God, let him live a few years longer." Her prayers were mixed with extreme anger at the driver of the red truck.

ANDREW

It was a carefree summer evening for Andrew, our youngest child; he had no particular responsibilities that night, so he and his wife, Shauna, met two other couples, Buddy and Ebeth and Floyd and Yvonne, and headed for Newport Beach. The weather was beautiful, the sea splendid. After spending a few hours there, they headed back to Rialto, all riding in the same car, and as they drove an interesting conversation developed. Some years before, one of Buddy's sisters had been involved in a fatal automobile accident. As they talked of it, Andrew suddenly said, "I don't think I could stand it if one my family were ever involved in a serious accident. I hope I never face such a thing."

When they got to Buddy's house, there was a note on Andrew's car window from Adam Pierce, Andrew's best friend. "Buck, call me," the note read. Andrew tried to reach him, but got no answer. Knowing we were scheduled to be home, he tried to call us. When he arrived at his own home, there was a crowd of church people milling around, and at that moment an ugly knowledge gripped him. Even before his friends told him the story, he knew something was seriously wrong. Inside his house, he checked his telephone for messages, heard Rick Manzer's voice, then called the hospital and talked to Steve.

"You need to hurry, Andrew. Dad is critically injured. The doctors don't know if he will live or not."

They left immediately, taking neither clothes nor a toothbrush. Adam was afraid for Andrew to drive, so while his wife, Sharon, drove the Pierce car, Adam drove Andrew and Shauna straight to the hospital. They talked every moment during the trip to Oxnard, as though words would dispel the ghastly vision in their heads. At times they felt faithless, fearful Andrew's father would die before they could arrive. Then they would rally, pull themselves together, and speak of God and His love and His power. Married and in their twenties, these young people had been taught all their lives to trust God. They had been told that He was sufficient, that He cared, and that He was real. Now, a quiz had been popped, a test scheduled.

It was nearing midnight when I saw Andrew coming down the hospital corridor. He walked slowly, his feet appearing to drag, as if he did not want to come. Shauna and his friends walked on either side, as though to prop him. Trembling, I embraced them all.

MICHAEL

When Michael hung up the telephone after talking to me he was panic stricken, feeling a sense of desperation and frustration. He was so far away, and it would take many hours before he could reach his dad's bedside. For a few moments, he slumped in his office chair, as he tried to gather his wits. He must decide on a course of action. Only a few months before, he had started his own business, Buxton Drywall, and of course, he was totally responsible for its operation. He relayed the situation to his foreman who spoke reassuring words to him. "Go to your dad. Everything will be fine here. I will personally see to it."

At home, Mike and Melina packed a small amount of clothes for themselves. Their children, Ryan and Kelly, were in Missouri visiting relatives, so no further arrangements would have to be made for them immediately. They took the necessary steps to close down their house, and made a few more phone calls to their friends, and to Melina's family. Mike shook with nervousness. He was frightened. "Please, God, do not let my dad die," he prayed. His hands were clammy.

Finally, they had made all the necessary arrangements. They had placed their things in the car, and were ready to leave. It was dark now. It was to be a long night as they flew over the highway system. Oxnard lay far to the west, many miles up the coast of California. It would take them six or seven hours to get there.

Michael did not have a cell phone, and throughout the long night as he sped toward us, he stopped to gulp coffee and to make frantic calls on pay phones. "How is he, Mom? Have there been changes?" I tried to calm Mike each time he called, and assured him that his dad was still alive.

It would be early on Sunday morning when Michael and his family arrived at the hospital, exhausted, and bleary-eyed. He was the last to arrive and we would embrace, and cry together.

5

They showed me to the room where we would wait while Jerry
endured his surgeries. The room began to fill, not only with our
children, but also with our friends. Several of them had been in Santa
Maria at the time of the accident, and they came quickly; others were
farther away, and it took longer for them to get to the hospital.

The waiting room was a typical one, and relatively comfortable.
It was furnished with numerous couches and chairs, lamps, and a desk
with a phone on it. Someone bought a notebook and stayed seated
by the telephone to record the many calls that were to come. People
pressed in until the room was filled, and chairs were set up in the
halls. "Please keep the center of the hall clear," a nurse said.

We prayed everywhere; we knelt and prayed, some went to the
chapel to pray, and preachers laid hands on me, asking God to let
Jerry live and to help me and give me strength. Men walked the
corridors. They prayed silently and they prayed aloud. When it was
appropriate, I asked preachers to go in to Jerry and to lay hands on
him. The late Kenneth Fields and Larry Alred were the first ones to
do so, having arrived shortly after the accident. "Are you sure these all
are preachers?" hospital personnel would ask me later.

"Yes, they are, and continue to let them in, please. It is important to us."

Dear friends looked deep into my troubled eyes. "We are with you; we are trusting and believing." They squeezed my hands and held me against the dark terror that cloaked me. Thus began an awareness of the loyalty and love of our friends that may only be described as astounding. The next few weeks would reveal extreme generosity and great personal sacrifice, a loving, remarkable gathering around a family who now faced days and nights of unspeakable grief, of bleak distress, of unanswerable questions. We were walking a strange path, an unknown and uncharted one, a path strewn with such boulders of trouble that the trouble itself become a material thing, generating its own negative life, and its own contrary force.

Members from our church in Rialto came and seated themselves for the long wait. Verlaine Walden was the wife of a colleague of Jerry's, and she was several months pregnant. Despite that, she and her husband came quickly and spent the entire night as we waited. The Wal-Mart across the street had a McDonald's that was open all night, and someone went over and brought back food to hand out. Paul Price, at that time the district superintendent of our church organization, was of inestimable strength to me. Sometime during the night, I walked through an adjoining room and found him hunkered on a short couch, trying to rest as we awaited the surgery's end.

This caring and loving response from our friends was not short-lived or fleeting. Throughout the weeks ahead, many that came to visit would take me out for a restaurant meal and would press dollars into my hand. For months, I drew no funds from our bank because of the generosity of our friends and their churches.

One day the late Paul Wilson called and said he wanted to come and bring me a gift. When he arrived he held a camera, and asked someone to snap a picture as he presented an envelope to me. I better understood the fanfare when I opened the envelope and read the amount of the enclosed check: *Ten thousand dollars*. At first, I could not speak; truly, I did not know what to say. This pastor had been so concerned about our situation that he spoke to his church in

Delano, CA.: "I would like you to give an offering to the Buxtons. Whatever amount this church gives, I will personally match it." When the ushers counted, there were five thousand dollars. As promised, he added five thousand, and presented the check to me.

We have tried to let these beautiful people know how much that meant; we have endeavored to thank them. In a faltering way, I did so then. We have spoken about it various times since, and Jerry and I have personally gone to their church to tell those tremendous saints and their blessed pastor how much we appreciate what they did. To this day though, I cannot get over this extreme and generous gift of love.

In addition, Steve was a full-time evangelist who depended completely on individual church offerings for his income. Understanding his unique situation, dear ministerial friends gave to him generously, enabling him to stay six or seven weeks in Oxnard. Later, when Steve and Dearrah calculated, they found their income during that time to have exceeded any other comparable period of travel. They gave some of the money to Andrew and Shauna so that they too could stay with their dad.

Throughout the five months Jerry was at St. John's local pastors visited literally every day, except for one, and many others who lived far often came to visit him. For weeks, the churches in the area sent food to the hospital for our meals, cards and letters came by the score, and flowers and plants were delivered to the waiting rooms.

It was reported by the hospital staff that in the first seventy-two hours, over one thousand phone calls came for us, and that the hospital called in an extra switchboard operator to handle the increased volume of calls. "Who is this person?" a hospital operator asked Larry Booker when he called, but could not get through to us because all the lines were busy.

"Just a man of God," he replied. He told us about it much later with a wide smile on his face.

Beginning that first Sunday and continuing for many weeks, Jerry's colleagues capably and willingly would fill his pulpit back in

Rialto. Several of our friends stayed in Oxnard for as long as a week. They checked into hotels, some even having their children with them. They stood by us, some verbal with their words of love and support, others saying little, but standing close—a shield, a guard…long day, and endless night.

Strangers ministered to us also, beginning with Lorraine Heter and Rick Manzer, and continuing now through caring hospital personnel. While still in the emergency waiting room, a chaplain came to comfort me, and a social worker came over. She supplied the private office for telephone calls, and inquired how she could further help. The doctors and nurses in the emergency room had been kind, and their demeanor spoke of sincere dedication and concern. After the initial surgeries, we would be shown to the ICU waiting room where we would settle in and spend several days. There were so many of us though, that it became a problem for others who waited also. One day a social worker came to discuss this with us.

"We have a room on the third floor that you might want to look at." He led me there, and it was wonderful. There were couches that folded out into beds, tables, and numerous chairs. Connected to that room was a kitchen, fully equipped with a stove, sink, table and chairs, and a refrigerator. "What do you think?" he asked.

"This is perfect. We will be comfortable here," I told him. "Thank you very much."

"Well, it's yours." Then he told me that only recently, a grieving family who had lost a child at St. John's had outfitted the room.

As we left the room, he tinkered with the telephone. "I will get a separate line working for you here." It seemed the word had spread throughout the hospital of the exceeding large number of phone calls we were receiving. Other hospital personnel supplied us with sheets, blankets, and pillows.

Sometime on that first Sunday, the social worker spoke with us, and while doing so, came to understand that our homes were a minimum of one hundred miles away. "Let me check something for you." He dialed a number, had a short conversation, and then told us the Doubletree Hotel in Ventura would be giving us three rooms for five nights, at no charge. What a blessing it was to have those rooms in which to refresh ourselves. Some of the family spent a few hours sleeping there.

James Bryson, a board member of our church, had a brother who lived in Oxnard. "They are going on vacation for a month and want you to use their home," he told us. Someone brought us the keys and gave us direction to their lovely home.

The nurses and doctors would prove to be exceptional people; people who cried with us, who laughed, and prayed, and worked, and struggled. Many months later as we arranged outpatient rehabilitation, Dr. Yu asked, "Where will you stay while you are in Oxnard?"

Jerry and I had talked about it and would schedule the weekly three days of therapy he must have in such a way that we would need to spend only two nights away from home each week. "We will stay in a motel," we told him.

`He looked at us intently, then shook his head, this great doctor who had become our friend. "There is no need for that; I have a beach home in Ventura, and you must stay there." Both of us felt awkward and sputtered objections, but he waved them away. "Let me run it by Mary Kay, then I'll bring you the keys." The next day he walked into Jerry's room, jingling the keys in the air as he handed them over. "Consider the home to be yours as long as you need it. There are groceries in the cupboard. Eat them," he finished with a huge grin.

A member of a church in Corona owned the Oxnard Wagon Wheel RV park, and when she heard of the accident, sent word that our motor home could be parked there for as long as we had need of it, and there would be no rent charged for the space. We parked it there for months, and when I was not staying at the hospital, that space was my home.

Waiting room strangers, eyes wet with their own tears, bodies stiff with unspeakable tension, bravely smiled at us and inquired, "How is your husband today?"

I would report the latest, then ask gently, "And you? Are things better?"

The road back was to be a torturous and grueling one. Perhaps in my subconscious I knew this as I waited that first night for the multiple surgeries to end. Around me, holding me erect with their strength was my family: my blood loved ones, my church family, and my extended one—humankind—who reached now to Jerry and to me.

The Family

The paintings of Norman Rockwell, the famed illustrator, are treasured for their vivid depiction of traditional life: a grandmother and small child praying over a café meal; a GI returned home, standing midst his city tenement, laundry flapping, his girlfriend and family rushing out; plump mom setting holiday bird on a festive table; the startled eyes of a boy as he pulls a Santa suit from a drawer; a coy young lady dressed in pink, preening for her first date. Family scenes pull at us, touch tender spots and precious vulnerable places. They evoke in us a primal response of warm connection that nourishes our own sense of community and of family. Our hands reach to the touch; our skin quivers with anticipation.

Ordained by God Himself, the family is the basic unit of society and is intended to nurture its young, providing food and shelter for them, while instructing them in the ideals that will enable them to successfully meet the challenges of life. Its role is to teach the work ethic and to instill a sense of moral responsibility within each person. Necessary in the atmospheric mix of the God-fearing home is true concern for others that encompasses care of the weak and injured and sincere respect and love for the aged. It is a place for the teaching of the Word of God. Moses explicitly directed the children of Israel:

"And these words, which I command thee this day, shall be in thine heart: And thou shalt teach them diligently unto thy children, and thou shalt talk of them when thou sittest in thine house, and when thou walkest by the way, and when thou liest down, and when thou risest up" (Deut. 6:6-7).

Many will agree that the moral declension in America is a reflection of the sad decay of its families, and that the rotting of this basic societal unit has virtually caused family training to vanish. Empty houses await the returning school child, while mothers hie away to work. There is no father, or at best his role is deprecated and sullied. Thus, family ideals are gone, as is a basic respect for authority and for simple morality. Those having authority often misuse it, lacking compassion and understanding. Space and purpose prevent full discourse on this subject, but these lines will serve to acknowledge the problem, to indicate the cause and the solution. Just as crucial—or more so, perhaps—is the pointing out of the opposite scenario. Not all is lost. There **are** families, strong families, God fearing ones—imperfect ones? yes, but striving-to-do-right ones. There are families who are hard workers, who care, who describe the way to their tender young, and who impose discipline on the wayward. There are still mothers who tend homes and fathers who lead.

Groups of similar passion naturally congregate, speaking to common goal, while honing and polishing their corporate purpose. Analyzing and refining their own skills and Calling, they join with others to effect their personal mission. The church is such an entity, peopled by those of Godly vision, forming a unique family. It is an earthy one, yet heavenly and of otherworld properties. It crosses denomination and bloodlines, ignores race and gender, and within its invisible walls allows no caste, nor work of segregation. Buildings do not describe the church, nor measure it, for its force presses against brick and mortar, flows through mullioned windows, and escapes into the street where it sweeps the gutter and washes through the suburbs. Its fountains gush to skyscraper—a flood gathering in the lost, the hurting, the needy. It is God's church, ruled and governed by Him, left in this world as light and salt: "…the general assembly, the church of the first born" (Hebrews 12:23). The church is a mighty army, a massive and conquering one, yet one who rallies to its weak, and to its downtrodden and hurting. It is an army who tramples not its injured, but who circles that one and tends his wounds. Indeed, such pause and such action speak to Calling and to Mission.

Narrow it would be, and foolish, to suppose that only through blood family and church family would come ministration and relief. Regardless of the undoubtedly accurate reports of callous disregard for human life and the riveting accounts that reveal streams of people who step over a dying man as he lies on city street, or the blatant disregard of dozens who hear a woman's scream for help, and that hours later is found murdered—despite these, let it not be forgotten that there is a caring, broad arm of humanity. We are common beings, lacking form, ethereal souls who jostle along, striving for the sense of our lives, needy and fragile and vulnerable. We come aware of our fellow and his life and struggle, so near our own, so like ourselves. A beloved story in the Bible is one Jesus Himself told. Recorded in the twelfth chapter of Luke is the account of a man who traveled from Jerusalem toward Jericho, and who fell among thieves that stripped him of his clothing, and who robbed and wounded him, leaving him half dead. It chanced that a priest and a Levite, both religious leaders, traveled that way, and when they saw the wounded man, they each in his time passed by, ignoring his need. Then came a Samaritan, a common man, who viewed his fellow with compassion, gathered him up, and tended his needs. Jesus castigated the former two, and set as example the lowly Samaritan, a Gentile who was viewed with disdain. Jesus plucked this fragment of life, lifting it high as a paradigm, a model. It graphically reveals the mighty arm, the wide reach of humanity.

So in our darkness, those infamous days in Oxnard, a family gathered and stretched its arms, each having its own role, each playing singular part. It was a holy stretch that took us in: God, my blood family, the church family, and the family of man.

The Struggle

"By the great force of my disease is my garment changed:
It bindeth me about as the collar of my coat."

Job 30:18

It was deep into the first night when Dr. Yu appeared in the doorway. I stood up, and when he began to speak, other people roused and pulled themselves together. Someone switched on a lamp as the doctor hoisted himself onto a gurney, swinging his legs a little as he spoke to us. The surgeries were finished, and Jerry had come through them reasonably well. His prognosis was grim though, and his odds for survival were poor. The next 24 to 48 hours were extremely crucial ones, but if he survived that long, there would be a chance for his ultimate recovery. Infection was his biggest enemy now, that being the leading killer of a patient who has initially survived such severe accident. The doctor also spoke of the possibility of his having a heart attack; a common reaction to such devastating damage as his body had endured. He would be taken directly from the surgical chambers to the Intensive Care Unit, where in two hours or so, his immediate family could see him.

Right away, we spoke to the doctor of our faith, voicing positive thoughts and our belief in God. The doctor responded in kind, seeming friendly and accommodating, and saying that Jerry would definitely need this kind of support from his family and from his friends. His thoughts were that these very qualities might contribute strongly to a patient's recovery.

We moved to the ICU waiting room, which was a few steps down the wide hall from the unit itself. It was a pleasant, airy room with large windows and comfortable furniture. There were not many other people there when we entered. Posted signs and brochures that we had been given informed us of ICU protocol, telling us such things as who could visit, the visiting times, services available, and what precautions should be taken. The phone on the wall was connected to the nurse's station inside the unit, and we were instructed that any person who wished to visit an ICU patient was to call first and get permission to enter.

Finally the two hours were up, and we could go in; Steve and I were the first to enter. The ICU was a large, essentially round room, laid out with the nursing station in the middle, individual rooms circling around. Each patient's room was visible from the nursing station. Telephones, computers, and additional workspace could be seen, along with the patient medical charts and other essential paraphernalia. A bluish-green glow emanated from a bank of screens; telemetry connected each patient to a monitor, programmed so that a strident alarm would sound should any vital function fall below set parameters. Jerry's room number was 17. They led us there, and I slowly walked to his bed.

Jerry's head was gargantuan, mummied down to the eyes in thick white cotton and swollen to such degree that he was hardly recognizable. I remember thinking that he looked considerably worse than he had in the emergency room. His body was grossly bloated, totally exposed, with only a small sheet thrown across his midsection. Nearly every inch of his body was covered with surgical bandages or was stuck through with needles. Drainage tubes snaked from his head, from his lungs, from his hip, and from his pelvis, gathering fluids into collection bottles near the floor and into pouches that lay beside him on the bed. Fresh blood was still transfusing him, and a superpubic catheter had been threaded into his bladder. One of his fingers glowed; a meter was clamped there, continuously gauging his oxygen saturation level. The respirator was hissing; a therapist sat at its controls marking a chart and calculating fresh adjustments.

I was aghast, never having seen anyone in such condition before. Steve stood stock-still, mute, staring. Then we rallied… and breathed again.

Eileen was his nurse. She told her name, and we introduced ourselves. She was cheerful and buzzed around as she took care of him. She talked to us freely and openly; explaining what she was doing as she went along. His condition and care appeared challenging and even overwhelming to me, but she acted as though it was nothing—only a routine job. She was tender and was obviously a caring nurse. However, she was not afraid of his fragile condition; she could handle this patient and nurse him to recovery. Her reaction helped us, and by the time we left the room, we had rebounded a little from our initial blow.

Steve and I talked to those who were still in the waiting room, describing Jerry's shocking condition. Only his immediate family were allowed to visit at this time, and of course none of us could be in his room long; certainly not all of us could be in there at the same time. After a while, however, all the family had been in, each one coming out completely stunned. Rebecca had gazed down at him, thinking that it was impossible for him to survive, then wondering what kind of life he would have if he did live. She felt he would not want to live in that condition, then she felt guilty for allowing such thoughts. Both Andrew and Michael felt they would collapse when they saw him, and they left the room quickly. It was a confusing time. None of us could stand to be in there, yet when we left, we needed to go back.

We took the basement elevator and walked around the corner to the cafeteria where we picked up orange trays and selected warm food to put in our quivering bodies. My food was oatmeal, gray and glutinous, and I pushed it around in the tan plastic bowl, taking few bites, but greedily drinking the scalding coffee I had poured. We were in pieces, a staggering infantry, lost and on enemy turf. We had listened to gunshots all night, and bombs; we had dodged, we had survived—all of us, but it showed. We were a ragged bunch. However, we were a determined bunch, and so we planned our survival.

For one thing, we must have clothes, and a toothbrush or two would be nice. Steve had a forty-foot trailer at the fairgrounds in Santa Maria, and of course, our motor home was there, so he, Greg, and Adam would drive up and bring those vehicles down to the hospital parking lot. Andrew, Shauna, and others of the family went to buy clothes and toiletries. Those of us who remained went back to the waiting room, and throughout the day, we went in to see Jerry as we could. After awhile, Mike and Melina went to the hotel to clean up and to get some rest.

8

It was during the middle of Sunday afternoon when one of the doctors came in the room and seated himself on the low table in front of me. "Mrs. Buxton, we have a problem. Your husband's kidneys are failing." The words he continued to speak were thoughtfully crafted and gentle, but when he had finished talking, I understood him to have suggested that our family should consider the possible necessity of long-term life support, and to decide under what conditions, and how long we would leave Jerry connected to machines.

It was an ominous sign, and I knew it; kidneys often shut down just before death. Yes, of course we would agree to dialysis if that would solve the problem. But life support? How long would we have machines breathing for him? Could we "pull the plug?" It was impossible for me to deal with such a subject at that time, and so I did not. I chose a different way, another mode. My family and friends who were there joined with me and we prayed—prayed that God would take over, that He would work in Room 17, and that Jerry's kidneys would begin to function again. The prayer was not long, probably did not sound too powerful, our voices were no doubt weak, but it was what we knew to do. Steve was still in Santa Maria picking up the vehicles, and I knew he would want to know this turn of events, so I spoke with him on the phone, telling him that the situation was grave. "Come as quickly as you can."

Steve was frantic now to get back to Oxnard. Friends dashed around and helped get his rig ready to move. John Noyes, a friend, felt it was just too much for Steve to drive, actually dangerous, given his anxiety level; instead, he would drive Steve down himself. Berl Stevenson was also back at the youth camp for a few hours, and when Steve told him of his dad's deterioration, Berl began shouting. He grabbed Steve by the shoulders and faced off to him. "He can't die. You hear me, Steve. He can't die." We had been close to the Stevensons for years. Our families had taken vacations together, traveling thousands of miles in our camping rigs. Often, we ate meals at the other's table; we worshipped together, and cried and laughed with each other. Many times Jerry has said that Berl was his best friend. Now, a friend lay dying. "He can't die, Steve. He just can't."

Some time had passed after that devastating conversation with the doctor when I picked up the ICU phone and asked if I could go in and see Jerry. The clerk checked with the nurse who said yes, I could come in. It was never easy to walk those few steps to his bed, so I steeled myself as I passed through his door. One thing that helped me tremendously was that I did not believe he would die: I never did think he would. (At the time I did not think of that as being faith, but in retrospect I see that it was, that God had given me a gift, a precious and timely gift—the gift of faith.) I stood beside him, silently looking on his body, at once so familiar to me, and again so completely foreign. The room was bright and noisy. In those early days at least one nurse was always there, often there were more, as well as technicians, lab workers, doctors, and people who cleaned the room. My mind buzzed as I looked at him. I'm not sure who the nurse was at this time, (it may have been Kathy), but she told me he was conscious and that I could talk to him. The bed was high, and being short, I had to stretch to be close to his face. I leaned close. "Jerry." He opened his eyes. "Jerry, I love you. You've been in an automobile accident, and you're in a hospital. But you will be all right. You're in Oxnard in a hospital." He closed his eyes, and I was not sure he heard me. "Jerry, you will be all right." I could not stay long. "I'm leaving now, but I will be back. All the children are here with me." I touched his arm, and kissed his face, and left the room.

It was perhaps two hours later when a doctor came again to where we waited. "Good news, Mrs. Buxton. His kidneys are functioning!"

I wish there were words to describe my feeling of relief at that moment. I wanted to cry, I wanted to slump down, I wanted to sink, but someone should yell, a cheer should be sounded. I think I smiled; I surely sighed and spoke ever-sincere words, "Thank you, God. Thank you, Jesus." The waiting room that a few hours before had resounded with prayer was now a temple of praise. Tears flowed and hands were raised in the air.[2] At that moment it was not ours to consider the others around us, their grief, their sorrow; it was ours to be thankful and to rejoice. We had dodged one more bullet.

Poor Steve. He could not know that Jerry had passed through this crisis. I felt for him and wished I could let him know, but he had no cell phone, and there was no way to contact him.

Steve was desperate. Sitting in the truck as John drove, he wanted to go ever faster. He had to get there, had to be there...his dad...his dad was dying. He must get to him before he died.

John found several empty parking spots not far from the hospital entrance. As soon as the engine stopped, they both jumped down and dashed into the hospital. Steve ran down the hall, slammed the up button of the elevator, and flew into the room where we sat.

He practically skidded on his knees before me, and I will never forget the look. His face was white, ashen as a corpse, set with brilliant eyes that flashed a fearful dread. His hair was tangled and wind-blown. "Mom! Dad...how is he?" He collapsed with relief on the floor as we told him the most recent development. As we basked in our remission, it was good that we did not know of the

---

[2] *We Pentecostals worship uniquely, praying both aloud and silently, sometimes raising our hands when we pray.*

life-threatening crises that would present themselves during the next
few days.

9

"This place is dangerous. You need to get out of the car." He had said that to her, he was sure of it.[3]

Then, stars off to the right, flashing lights, and a dark whirling, a sucking down, a tunnel.

"Hang on, Jerry, you're going to make it." Someone had said that. He was positive he had heard it.

He couldn't get air, then a sharp thing jabbed at him, and he could breathe.

He was gray, wrapped in wool, muffled, and painless. It was dark though. His eyes—were they open or shut? He slept. He was not.

"Cough," someone said. "Cough again." Something was in his throat, a stick stuck down. A sucking noise was at his ear. "Cough, Mr. Buxton."

He slept. He was not.

"Jerry. I love you, Jerry."

---

[3] *These are his own impressions, but Jerry does not recall the time nor sequence of them.*

10

By Monday morning, the vehicles had been parked; all of us had bathed, eaten a regular meal, and had dressed in fresh clothes. We felt refreshed. Most of us stayed at the hospital around the clock those first few days, leaving only for short periods of times, then quickly returning. We knew we were in for the "long haul" and that we had to take care of ourselves, so we tried to sleep a little and to eat proper meals.

Now we had time to talk at length about Jerry's condition, of the challenges we could expect, and about the changes that had come to our lives. We counted our blessings though; he was still alive, and I specifically recall saying how glad I was that he did not have a broken neck, and that he was not paralyzed. Our family is quite an active one, and when our boys had started climbing trees and riding bicycles and motorcycles, it scared me. Jerry had told me to relax. "Let them be boys." I had learned to do so fairly well, I believe, but one of my on-going fears, especially when they rode motorcycles, was that one of them would sustain a head injury and become paralyzed. "Wear your helmets. Always," I nagged. I was grateful that the X-rays of Jerry's neck had shown no fractures.

It was either late Sunday night or early Monday that Ann Kelley, a blood specialist, was called in. Jerry's latest lab sheets reported an ominous drop in his platelet count, putting him at immediate risk of severe hemorrhage. Dr. Kelley concurred with the concerns of the attending physician, her consultation report saying that a "disseminated intravascular coagulation like syndrome certainly could occur, particularly in the presence of multiple deep bone fractures and almost inevitable fat emboli." [4]

If hell has rooms, then this one surely was designed there: the little one off the ICU waiting room where they take families to tell them the dreadful news. I came to hate the place. Whenever a doctor would come and ask to see us there, my legs would turn to sea foam, and I doubted they could carry me that far.

On Sunday, it had been his having a fresh bleed into his brain; a subarachnoid hemorrhage.[5]

On Monday, it was Dr. Kelley.

On Tuesday, it was Dr. Chieu, a kidney specialist. His message: Acute renal insufficiency again, with the likelihood of Jerry's needing to be placed on a kidney machine within the next 24-72 hours.

On Wednesday Dr. Yu told us he had a high fever, and that he had increasingly severe pneumonia. A sheet that circulated cold water was placed under his burning body.

Also on Wednesday, Dr. Chieu and Dr. Yu agreed that the possibility of sepsis[6] must be considered.

During one of our visits to the "hell room", one of the doctors spoke to us of adult respiratory distress syndrome[7], telling us that Jerry was at a very high risk of developing this condition because of

---

[4] *Disseminated intravascular coagulation is a condition in which small blood clots disseminate through the bloodstream, blocking small blood vessels and depleting the clotting factors needed to control bleeding. It is a life threatening condition.*

[5] *A subarachnoid hemorrhage is sudden bleeding into the space between the brain and the lining that surrounds it. One third of people who have such a hemorrhage die immediately. This type of bleeding is evidence of very severe brain injury and is associated with long-term brain damage.*

the extremely large amount of blood he had received. His hospital charts reveal that before this ordeal was over he had received at least thirty-nine units of blood, which is nearly four times the amount a typical adult has circulating through his vascular system. By Monday, he had also received fifteen units of packed red cells, and seven units of fresh frozen plasma. He was bleeding so fast in the emergency room that they did not have time to do the sub-matching of his blood; we were warned that other serious problems could arise from that.

Once, Berl went with us into the dreaded room, and when the doctor finished telling of the latest deadly development and had gone from us, Berl raged at me, "I don't even want to keep a motor home, Shirley. I don't want one if Jerry dies. Who would I travel with?" We were bags of emotion, rattling through each day, raspy and shivering at night, as we walked the halls and into his room, and back out again. We had moved to the third floor waiting room, one that gave us much more privacy than had the regular ICU waiting room. In the evenings, we would spread out the beds and take turns resting on them.

We kept our heads by a strong, unyielding faith in God, coupled with our personal strengths, and by a force we surely created as we linked up, directing as a single entity our thoughts and prayers to God—the Almighty, the Omnipotent great One. He could do it. We believed Him. After all, He had created Jerry and knew him intimately. Surely, He could heal his fractured and sick body. We supported each other; our friends held and steadied us. We wept. We prayed. We tried to smile.

Steve went across the street to Kinko's and had a large banner made. He brought it into the hospital, got tape somewhere, and mounted it over the door directly in Jerry's line of vision. It read:

---

[6] *Sepsis is an infection in the bloodstream, a serious development with a high risk of death.*

[7] *Adult respiratory distress syndrome is a type of lung failure resulting from many different disorders that cause fluid accumulation in the lungs. One of its known causes is a high volume of blood transfusions.*

"It is of the LORD's mercies that we are not consumed, because his compassions fail not" (Lamentations 3:22). In one of his times of meditation, this scripture had been impressed on Steve, and he felt that he should post it in his dad's room. It remained there until the day Jerry was discharged. Then we carried it with us to rehab and stuck it on the wall there. Cards were coming in now, and we also taped them up for him to see.

Eileen and Kathy, his two primary nurses, showed us how the morphine pump worked. "If he seems to be suffering, push this button."

"You've been in an accident, Jerry. Do you remember?" we frequently said. "You're in Oxnard, and we're all here with you." From the beginning, he remembered and would nod ever so slightly. We read scriptures aloud to him and took a tape player in to play music. By this time, a few preachers had been allowed in to see him and to pray with him. Later, many of them told us that after they saw him, they did not expect him to survive.

11

It was Thursday evening of week one, and as I walked into the unit, a nurse spoke to me. "Mrs. Buxton, Dr. Herman is on the phone and wants to talk with you. You may take the call here." I had never met Dr. Herman, so it seemed unusual that he would ask to speak to me. Instantly my legs became of the sea foam, made-in-hell-room variety, and they did not want to move. Nevertheless, they did; I forced them. The doctor sounded young, and his voice was of a pleasant tone, but his style was hesitant, as though he could easily lapse into a stutter. I could hear the concern in his voice. During the recent few hours, Jerry had become less mentally aware, was lethargic, and now was losing the ability to move his arms and legs. They had done a CAT scan and now must do a cervical myelogram to pinpoint the problem. As though bewitched, I hung up the telephone.

My head was shot through with silver, a silent roar that came at me and took me. I was still; I swallowed hard, took short breaths, feeling my nostrils flare, and walked into his room. He looked the same. His head was wedged now though, a large sandbag on either side, holding his skull straight and unmovable. His eyes were closed. However, when I walked closer, he opened them, though, perhaps not seeing me. His left eye jerked in a back and forth motion, a condition the doctors called nystagmus. This development had alarmed his medical staff.

Dr. Herman performed a procedure in which he inserted a needle into Jerry's spinal canal at the level of L3-4; the spinal fluid that came out of the needle was blood tinged when it should have been clear. Continued testing revealed a fracture of his neck at C6. There was also a bone fragment at C5, with a moderate widening of the anterior epidural space at approximately the C3 level; this extended far down his spine to the C7-Tl level. This was a terrible discovery. The spinal cord itself had been damaged; the tests showed significant swelling, most noticeable in Jerry's upper cervical spine at levels above C5. An epidural hematoma was clearly visible, most pronounced at the C2 level.[8] He was returned to his bed in the ICU where Dr. Herman followed him.

The existing bandages were removed from Jerry's head, and preparations were made to place him in a halo brace. His head was prepped and draped, then four pin sites were shaved and numbed with Xylocaine. Once this was done, a halo ring was placed and pins were inserted into his skull. The remainder of the halo brace was then connected. He was outfitted in a large vest; from that came steel rods that held the apparatus in place. His head was now rigid and immobile.

Dr. Herman spoke with us, expressing his sorrow at this development. The doctors had looked again at the X-rays taken on Saturday when Jerry was first admitted, but for some reason, his broken neck did not show on those films. Dr. Herman could not predict how much movement Jerry would eventually regain in his limbs. Considering his severe spinal injuries, there was a strong possibility that he would remain a quadriplegic. "Let us hope for the best, though," he said.

---

[8] The 8 cervical, 12 thoracic, and 5 lumbar nerves, are numbered as to where they emerge from the spinal cord.

"Here, Mr. Buxton. I'm going to suction you. We must keep those lungs clear." Someone gagged him, and his shoulders heaved, though no sound came.

"Cough, Mr. Buxton. Try to cough."

He blinked his eyes and saw a clock and a sign—what was that sign? Fuzzy. Can't read it. What is the day? What time does that clock say? Is it night or day? I'm in a hospital. They told me that. I remember. I have been in an accident.

Cough.... Suction... Cough...Suction

He closed his eyes. He slept. He was not.

"Your family is here. They want to see you."

His head felt strange, heavy. Uncomfortable. He needed to turn it. It was stuck. What was wrong? Why couldn't he move his head?

"Cough. Here, I'm going to suction you." Someone gagged him again.

He slept. He was not.

His nose itched, and he would scratch it. He lifted his hand...his hand, lift. Why couldn't he lift his hand? What was wrong? Maybe he was asleep. Where was he? What was going on, anyway?

He saw Shauna. He winked at her.

13

It was Friday, August 13, and this was Chris Mears' wedding anniversary, but he had been kind enough to come anyway. Thinking we might need legal advice, one of our friends had highly recommended that we consult with him, so he had driven from Orange County to Oxnard that day. Most of our family were there, and we had been introduced and were now sitting around a table in a third floor conference room. Someone tapped on the door. "Dr. Herman wants to see you in the ICU." We looked at each other, then, as though fated and resigned to uncertain and unpleasant destiny, we pushed our chairs back and rose. We escorted Mr. Mears to the waiting room close by, introduced him to friends, and excused ourselves. Down the hall we walked, a dirge, a circumscribed inevasible journey. Would this never end?

Dr. Herman's piercing blue eyes speared us through as he spoke. Their most recent tests revealed that despite the halo, Jerry's cervical spine still showed signs of gross instability, and that overnight, the space between C5 and C6 had widened. "Mr. Buxton's fractured neck is unstable. We must do surgery immediately." Dr. Herman's startling blue eyes were kind. "I am sorry. Really, I am." The clerk gave me papers to sign.

"How much can a body take?" I asked once back in the waiting room. "How much more can he stand?"

Dan Walden seemed to soothe the tension in the room. "Let us be thankful for what we have. Your husband's accident was six days ago. Today, we could have been attending a funeral."

Under a general anesthetic, Jerry's neck was opened and the instability was recognized immediately. The anterior ligament was found to be torn, and the posterior ligament was ripped completely. A disc was removed. There were signs of a cerebrospinal fluid leak as well, prompting Dr. Herman to state in his surgical notes that the dura, a membrane that covers the spine and the brain, was likely open. He fastened two screws into the body of C5 and C6 to repair the fracture; the surgery was finished.

Dr. Herman came out to tell us that Jerry had tolerated the surgery well, that all we could do now was wait. Dr. Herman mentioned that he was leaving the next day for his annual vacation, and that one of his colleagues would do the follow-up on Jerry. Though in the midst of his vacation, this kind man called during the next few days to inquire about Jerry's condition.

Since he could not move, the medical staff placed Jerry on a bed that rotated, so that over the course of an hour, in small increments, his body was turned from side to side. His feet were down pointing, so podus splints were prescribed to hold them straight and in a natural position. The halo was large and ugly. He was still on the respirator, of course, but his blood condition had stabilized, and he was not receiving any more transfusions. Sometimes when we went in to see him, he was awake; more often during these days he seemed to be sleeping.

Michael was very concerned about his business, and though it was a hard decision, he felt he must return to Arizona. Although his friends and colleagues had pitched in to run the crews while he was in Oxnard, he knew the fledgling business really needed him. In addition, Kelly and Ryan would be coming home in a few days, and Michael and Melina must be there for them.

He went in to see his dad before he left, and told him, again, how much he loved him. "You're a survivor, Dad! I know you will make it." He would stay in frequent contact. Jerry seemed to understand. It was an emotional time as Mike said good-bye to his siblings and to me. We had been through a lot these last few days; we had faced death head on, and together we had endured.

14

Many friends had offered to fill Jerry's pulpit, so we knew it would not be hard to schedule a preacher for each service. On Sunday, the eighth day after the accident, Steve and I drove to our church in Rialto. Our district superintendent thought it would be good if I could go to our church weekly and be with our people, at least for the morning services; he had strongly encouraged me to do so if I felt I could manage it at all. They were needy and hurting too, their pastor had been stricken, and it could have a steadying effect if I, at least, were there. It is approximately one hundred miles from Oxnard to Rialto, and is quite a pleasant drive. I knew that I should go, and I desired to be there, yet I felt apprehensive as we drove, knowing surely that it would be an emotional gathering.

It was, but I faced it. As I stood behind the podium to speak, I was completely honest, telling them of Jerry's critical injuries and of his poor prognosis. Nevertheless, I spoke in a positive way. I wept as I told them Jesus was our comfort. I was weak, so I reminded them of the strength of God. I faltered, but told them that Jesus is a lifter of the head. The entire service was of great strength to me; it eased and refreshed me. The sound of the worship and its familiar feel was as balm gently applied to searing skin. I cannot repeat the words of the sermon, but I recall that they ministered to me, infusing me with a calm serenity, and I know I received more in that service than I possibly could have given.

After church, we went to my home where I gathered clothes and other things I might need, including insurance papers. From one of our files, I drew our insurance booklet.

In the evening, we had a fight. At the hospital. With a doctor. Some of the children and I had been in Jerry's room to see him, and we were standing in the unit near the nurse's station when a doctor approached us and began talking of Jerry's condition. She had assisted Dr. Herman with the neck surgery, and he had asked her to do the follow-up, as he was to leave shortly thereafter on his vacation. We were astonished at what she said. I do not remember her exact words, but she was inexorably pessimistic, and she did not smile. She seemed malevolent and gave us no hope for his recovery. We rejected her. I spoke up, and my response in turn seemed to astound her; well do I remember her reply. "Mrs. Buxton, your husband is sixty-two years old, and his wide range of extremely severe injuries is such as to kill a much younger person, much less someone of your husband's age. Do you not know that?" I was appalled. We were all appalled.

"But what of faith?" we asked. "We believe in God, and we trust Him. Does that not count; is not faith a force? Surely that gives us some hope." All of us joined in the conversation, and although I cannot recall our exact words, or the rest of hers, as the conversation developed, it became clear that we were at odds with this doctor and her philosophy. She no doubt felt the same about us.

She bristled, and after a brief further exchange of words, she turned and left us—a huddled group, reeling from the blow we had been punched. Steve immediately went to the nursing supervisor. After telling her of the incident, he informed her that our family did not want to talk with that particular doctor again. The supervisor said she understood, and the hospital would abide by our wishes.

Later, there were occasions when we talked to other doctors about this incident, and without exception, each of them, said she was

an excellent doctor, although acknowledging her poor "bedside man-
ners". "If one of my children had need of a neurosurgeon," one of
them said to me, "I would choose her." However, they did seem to
understand our situation and our position. We never had occasion to
speak with that doctor again, although at times, we passed her in the
halls and sometimes she would nod. I hope we were not too hard on
her; I do not think we were.

In contemplating that day, given our plight and our grave state
of mind, I believe we did the wisest thing. We had been honest
with ourselves and with each other, and we knew that Jerry might not
survive. He had massive injuries, and we reckoned with his not being
a young man. We wrestled with questions: If he did live, would he
walk? Would he ever breathe on his own? Was he to be bound to
a wheelchair? These were serious and pertinent questions; it was we
who had to deal with them. We chose to surround ourselves with
positive and heartening people, people who would believe with us and
who conceivably could speak the word "miracle." We had to speak
faith. We had to breathe faith. There was room for nothing else.

15

We settled into a comfortable routine—at least as comfortable as one can be in such a situation—and as the days passed, we became increasingly aware of what a fine hospital St. John's was. We had few complaints, truly feeling that Jerry was getting the best care possible. His nurses were the finest, and they seemed genuinely interested not only in his recovery but in our comfort and health as well. They marked well each small step that he took toward recovery: a nurse yelled excitedly one morning as she came down the unit telling the whole place that one of his basic bodily functions had returned. Our faces were red at the words she used, but our hearts leaped at the progress. The nurses were kind and seemed in tune with us, appearing to buy into our trust in God and our overall philosophy of life.

A preacher was visiting one day, and as was our habit, before he left, we stood close by the bed and touched Jerry as we prayed for him. That day we had joined hands. Eileen, his nurse, pressed into the circle, grasping a hand, and said, "Let me pray too." We loved her for it. The staff recommended restaurants and shopping areas and admonished us to take care of ourselves. Eileen was from Great Britain, and she told us of a place in Ventura that was like an English pub, and she even told us what to order when we went. One of our favorite places was just across the street—a bistro called Mario's.

Once in the early days, I was pleased and a little surprised to find a physical therapist with Jerry, and although Jerry was hardly able to move, the therapist gently massaged his hands and flexed his fingers. Later, the therapists would slowly lift his arms and put them down, and raise and lower his legs.

We had been out to dinner on one occasion and when we returned, the hospital was dark. We did not learn the exact cause of the power outage, but we were told the emergency generator had been powered up and was supplying enough energy to run the essential equipment. The elevators were not considered essential equipment though, and we had to climb the stairs to reach Jerry's floor. Later in the evening, the emergency generator failed for a short time also, and several patients on respirators had to be hand ventilated. The staff, patients, and families remained calm, and the situation was always under control; however that night, Steve had a nightmare in which his dad must be rescued from some kind of catastrophe, and Jerry had hallucinations and dreams of deadly earthquakes. One of the generators was located close to the head of his bed, separated only by a wall, and it quite naturally frightened him that its humming sound was missing. The hospital personnel handed out lanterns for us to use while navigating the dark halls.

We stayed with Jerry as much as we could, but there was so much going on with his treatment and with his daily care that much of our time was spent in waiting rooms. Steve's boys, Chris and Joel, were sixteen and fifteen, respectively, and it was understandable that they were sometimes bored. Once as we waited, Chris, in a playful motion, fell onto the floor, as though in a faint. We laughed and continued with our reading and conversation until a security guard walked into the room. "Is everything all right?" We looked puzzled. Yes. Everything was fine. In response to our confusion, the guard told us that on the internal monitoring system he had observed Chris fall onto the floor and wondered if he had been hurt. We yelped with laughter. From then on, we kept out a wary eye for secret cameras; we scanned every corner, especially considering them when we folded out our beds on the third floor. The boys wanted to convince their dad to let them go surfing, so we secretly got out a piece of paper, and I wrote a prescription for a beach trip. I drew a line at the bottom of the page, wrote DOCTOR underneath it, and sent them to find a doctor who would sign it. They came back grinning, the authorized signature plainly written, at least as plainly as doctors are apt to write. Steve said, okay, okay, they could go surfing.

There were also many matters of business to which to attend. My boys had gone to retrieve the Landcruiser, but it could not be released to them, and they came to tell me I would have to go with them to claim it. During the trip to the storage yard, I found myself agitated, and I remarked that riding in the traffic was alarming and caused me to feel unsafe and vulnerable. In addition, I felt uneasy about seeing the vehicle. However, it really did not look too bad; unfortunately, Jerry himself had taken the biggest blow.

And then there were the more mundane things: there were personal bills to pay, and I was somewhat concerned about our house sitting empty and thought someone needed to care for the lawns. I bought a telephone and had a line installed in our motor home at the RV park so that I could stay in touch with the hospital when I wasn't there, and with the church family in Rialto. The church itself must be looked after. There was a lot to consider.

I had given our medical membership number to Chris Mears, and a call came from him giving me the disconcerting word that our health insurance excluded coverage for automobile accidents. I was surprised and alarmed, as our automobile policies had a very small coverage for medical expenses. Thinking perhaps there had been a mistake, I personally checked the handbook I had taken from our files a few days before. I read it through and understood the awful truth: We had no coverage. Frank had a suspended driver's license, no automobile insurance at all, and after Mr. Mears ran an asset check on him, found that he also had no money.

What was I to do? How would I pay these enormous hospital bills? The mere thought of it was overwhelming, but I remember discussing it with my children and telling them I just could not worry about it. "If they boot us out of the hospital, we will circle around Daddy and his hospital bed on the parking lot." I knew that would not happen, but what actually would occur and what the solution was, I could not know.

Soon a social worker came to me and brought papers, suggesting that I apply for Medi-Cal. She was a thoughtful lady, and from day to day would stop by to talk with me. I had little hope of any government assistance though, for we were middle-class people, owned a home and cars, and had a small amount of money in savings. It was the responsible thing that we had provided for ourselves as we were not far from retirement age, but we absolutely did not have enough money to pay the medical bills of the amount that surely were accumulating. I recalled conversations that I had heard and magazine and newspaper articles that had given me the understanding that only the destitute would qualify for such help. Would we now be penalized for being responsible adults? Is it better in such a case to have nothing, to have not worked or saved for the future? In the days and weeks to come, as I worked through this situation and attempted to solve it, I would agonize over it. But for now, I actually did not, as I recognized that there was absolutely nothing I could do.

By now, after talking to hospital personnel, I had an idea that Jerry would be in the hospital for many weeks, perhaps even months. Knowing the rate of hospital charges, I knew that we were facing a bill that easily could run into hundreds of thousands of dollars. Had it been a much lesser amount we needed, I might have let my mind dwell there, for I would have considered my options in raising the money. Realistically though, the amount we would need was far beyond our resources, so I chose not to worry about it at that time. I would do what I could, but I truly would leave it in the hand of God. He would direct us.

Room 17 was not without its moments of gaiety and laughter. Among ourselves, we had resolved to smile when we walked in and, generally, to be as upbeat and positive as we possibly could. We would not speak of our fears, nor in his presence, speak of Jerry's poor prognosis; neither would we mention the challenges of the long-distance managing of the church or of the disruption of our own lives and its attending distress. Those were not hard decisions; they were natural conclusions. We chose to make happy faces and to infuse him with as much positive energy as we could. We held the ten thousand-dollar check close to his eyes and told him about the great things that were happening. We read aloud the funny cards and told him of the telephone calls that came from all over the country and of the multitude of friends who were visiting. Although it was recorded by one of his favorite singers, we decided one of the tapes sounded too mournful and melancholy. "He doesn't need to hear that kind of music right now," we decided, taking the cassette out of the room. We laughed and joked with the nurses and with each other.

Some of the humor came from the person on the bed. He was awake more now, and one of the immediate challenges was understanding him when he tried to communicate, as he was still on the respirator and had to mouth words around the tube. It was hard to make out what he was saying. We felt sorry for him, as we would repeat what we thought he was saying, and no, that was not it. Sometimes he would give up, and we never knew at that time what he wanted to tell us. "Turkey on a string," he said one day. Turkey on a string? Is that what you're saying? "Yes." We looked at each other, baffled, then we grinned across the bed as he settled down and said no more; and we were sure that was what he had wanted us to know. Very revealing and important information. One day he said some hilarious things—hilarious and of the family stories variety, and it is probably best that we keep the details to ourselves. He was so funny, and we wanted to hoot, but he was so sick, and so hurt, that we tried to restrain ourselves, merely smiling then, but howling once we got in the waiting room. (We still howl about the things he said when we get together, and he gets a sheepish grin on his face.)

Once when I went in, he looked frantic and immediately began trying to talk to me. It was terrible as I strained to understand him, for I could see he was immensely distressed. Finally, I understood him.

"I need $5,700.00. I must have it, or they are going to kill me."

Gently, I spoke, telling him that he was badly injured and that perhaps things were not as he perceived them. This was a good hospital, and they were giving him excellent care. He would not be calmed, but begged me to take him to a hospital near our home. "Take me to Loma Linda. Please, Shirley. They're trying to kill me here." I tried to soothe him, explaining again the situation, and saying he needed to trust me.

His reply was pitiful: "I don't trust you."

Later in the day, Steve and Berl came to see him, and immediately he told them the same story. He must have that money or they were going to kill him. They were wiser in dealing with him than I had been, saying, "Don't worry. We'll get the money for you." He was satisfied and never mentioned it again.

We did everything we could think of to make his room pleasant and to make him happy and comfortable. Our friend Holly, who is a nurse, said we should bring a picture of him so the staff would see it and think of him in that way, instead of only as a banged up patient. With tape, we stuck a recent picture onto his IV pole, right beside a well-dressed stuffed monkey who had chosen that spot to live. Rebecca rubbed him with lotion, and we told him we loved him, that God loved him, and that he was getting better.

An intensive care unit can be a frightening place; one day three people died, and the sadness of those families gushed over us. We were fellow travelers, we had talked together as we waited turns to visit, and we ached for them. I believe we would relate and be sympathetic at any time, but it was especially so now. We were raw and vulnerable ourselves, and that knowledge never ventured far from our consciousness. We recognized our mortality; we had handled it and had touched it. It had ventured too close. Andrew, especially, was disturbed when patients in the unit died.

"Cough, Mr. Buxton."

Cough…Suction…Cough…Suction.

I can't move; I'm captured, and in the night, those people came to me. They told me they were going to kill me if I don't get the money. They mean it too. They rolled out caskets and showed them to me, pushed them up and down the hall.

"Mr. Buxton, we're going to take more X-rays."

Cough…Suction…

I think that was Brother Price. Was he here to visit me? I know I'm sick and in the hospital. Oxnard, I think.

She's grinning. Who? That woman. The one in the clock. She sits inside there and looks at me and grins. She comes out sometimes, out of the clock that is. She has red hair, and her face is freckled. "You can do this," she says. Is she talking to me? "You can wrap around the wall, too. Look." She leaves the clock and slides along the wall, slithering, high, near the ceiling. She is part of the wall, melds into it.

"Jerry. Hi! How are you feeling today?"

Money, Shirley. I've got to have that money.

Cough…Suction…

Sleep. Awake. Sleep.

There is the ship, and I believe that is Brother Gray on it, but what of this line in my nose? Poison, that's what it is. Someone told me they would run the poison down this line into my body.

Cough…Suction.

Did Shirley smile? What is so funny?

"You can get in the wall, too."

Am I awake or asleep? Were they here? Who? That ship—where is it?

It's daytime, and Shirley is here. She needs to get rest. She has circles under her eyes. This must be so hard on all of them. I'm scared. I can't move. It was the accident, I know now. I'm paralyzed. I need to talk. Why can't they understand me?

In God will I put my trust.

My legs hurt. I need to be moved. That young nurse left me on my side, and my legs are hurting. I can't speak to tell her, and they're hurting so badly. Where is she? Please come. Please, let her come.

In God will I put my trust.

"Mr. Buxton, we're going to take your respirator tube out today."

17

We had turned the corner. Nobody announced just when it was, but we knew. We had made the turn. He **was** going to live. The atmosphere was lighter, the flowers in the planters had gone from muted, muddied gray to vibrant, shouting colors, while overhead the sky had blazed into a brilliant indigo blue. Our smiles were less and less of the must-do-it, stuck on kind, and our haunted, drawn looks gave way to sparkling eyes and glowing faces. Shauna, Dearrah, and Rebecca found consignment stores and went shopping; all of us were more relaxed and felt comfortable enough to leave for a few hours.

Although Jerry continued his deadly struggle, he was making great strides; many of the drainage tubes were gone and fewer bottles now hung by the bed. TPN is a yellow/green nutritional liquid, and it was one of the IV bottles that remained. They weaned him from the respirator, and he received his oxygen now through a cannula in his nose.

It was Friday the 19th, exactly one week following his neck surgery, when they prepared to get Jerry out of the bed for the first time. Therapists joined with the nursing staff, pulling a cardiac chair alongside his bed, a chair that actually was flat and looked like a gurney. I was in the room and watched. It took four people to transfer him, and once they had him moved, the bed folded in such a way that it became a chair. He sat upright now, connected still to oxygen, the halo holding his head erect, and with all his tubes dangling. He wobbled and smiled, then began complaining of pain. His voice was raspy, and he spoke softly and in a breathy way. His shoulder was hurting and finally the pain was so intense he was in tears, so they put him back to bed; new tests would show that his shoulder was dislocated.

Another day, as he sat in the chair, the nurse spoke. "You will get food today." I watched as she fed him Jello. It was red, and jiggled around in the spoon. It was beautiful; we were happy. He swallowed and did not choke.

Within hours, he had a burning fever and was struggling to breathe. "What is wrong," I asked a nurse.

"We are not sure," she replied. He had battled pneumonia from the beginning, and there were bacteria in his blood. They continued with his treatments.

They fed him soup, also, and he called it delicious. He swallowed; he did not choke. We were happy.

His fevers continued to spike, so Dr. Yu performed a bronchoscopy. Then he asked to speak with me concerning the results. He had found Jerry's vocal cords to be damaged, perhaps paralyzed, and that any food he ate was going directly into his lungs and not into his stomach. (One of the functions of the vocal cords is to guide food into the stomach.)

"What can we do," I asked

At least for the time being, he would not be able to eat or drink anything by mouth, and he would need a surgical procedure to have a gastrostomy tube placed, through which he would be fed[9].

On September 1, Dr. Sanchez and Dr. Rotenberg came to his bed in the ICU, where they prepared him for the surgery. They cut the harness part of the halo brace in order to gain access to the place

---

[9] *Nutrients are fed through this tube, which is surgically inserted into the stomach through the abdominal wall.*

where they would make the incision, and then they inserted the tube. The staff would observe him, then in 24 hours, the G-tube feedings would begin. Jerry was very disappointed, as were we all, but we merely tucked this challenge into the large bag we already had, stirred it around, and reminded God of our faith and trust in Him, and of our absolute dependence on Him.

Exercise was important to Jerry, as was a change of scenery, so one day when he was up in his chair, Kathy took him on a trip around the unit, actually going through the doors into the hall outside the unit, then making a circle and back in again. We trailed along, a family parade. There should have been marching bands with trumpets and bass drums, and glistening tubas; stallions wanted to prance and snort and paw. There must be cavorting clowns and roaring cannons. Cotton candy, pink and puffed up clouds of sugar, should have been in our hands and smeared on our faces. It was surely a day for celebration. Although it was only for a moment, the ICU had been left behind. Though he must return for awhile, he had, at least briefly, vacated that room, going not again to surgeon's knife, but to riding of parade, a parade of triumph and of joy. Many had feared he would never leave Room 17 alive; now those hellish thoughts were squashed and cast out.

The therapist said that I should bring in tennis shoes for Jerry, and they would put those on him instead of the podus splints. I bought size twelves, as his swelling was still so severe that his regular size tens would have been much too small. When I first saw him lying in the bed with those tennis shoes on, it startled me, and I did not like seeing them. I was puzzled about my reaction, but after thinking about it, concluded that to me the podus splints were connected to sickness, a patient, a temporary, fleeting condition; whereas Jerry's wearing tennis shoes in bed had a connotation of permanence, of nursing homes, and of unknown qualities and disabilities.

The social worker that had spoken with me about Medi-Cal came more frequently now and strongly suggested that I have a formal meeting at one of their offices there in the hospital. Understandably, the hospital wanted to do all they could to help me pay these bills; they had a lot at stake, a big investment in us now. I scheduled the meeting and gathered the papers they told me to bring. When the time of the meeting came and I waited for them to call my name, I felt embarrassed and humiliated. Neither Jerry nor I had ever applied for public assistance, and it did not sit well with me that I must do so now. My ears roared, my heart forged, then they called my name and I went in. I presented my papers: the list of our assets, investment papers, bankbooks and statements, registration slips from our automobiles, the deed to our home, mortgage papers, documentation of income, and such. I was frightened and felt muddled, as though I could not concentrate.

The worker scrutinized my paper work and told me to get everything out of Jerry's name. She selected certain annuities and suggested I cash them in. Perhaps if we could pauperize Jerry we could get some help with the bills. I detested it, and my mind revolted, but there seemed nothing else to do. The worker who was advising me was an employee of the state and told me frankly I might do everything she was suggesting and still not receive any assistance. It was my only hope, though.

I hired an attorney who specialized in these things, went to her office, laid out my papers again, and told her what I had been advised. She said that seemed right to her, but I sensed she really did not know what to tell me. She spoke extensively about the complexity of social security regulations and how different people may interpret them in different ways. She wanted payment on the spot, so I wrote her a check for $500.00 and did not consult with her again.

I began the frustrating job of taking my husband's name off his bank accounts, off his car registration, and off the home he had bought through his hard work, and was paying for. It was a nightmare.

There was much better news in Jerry's room however, for they had begun to talk of releasing him from the ICU and of transferring him to a rehabilitation unit. Dr. Judy, the head of the rehab department, had come in to visit Jerry and had done a complete analysis, mainly to ascertain whether or not Jerry had enough potential to be accepted in their program. Good news. Yes, they would take him.

There was a question in my mind about the best place to take him for rehab, and I discussed the options with my family and close friends, and, to an extent, with Jerry himself. What seemed ideal was that we take him to a rehab hospital near our home in Rialto, but the problem was our lack of insurance, whereas St. John's was willing to accept him even with our financial problems. In addition, we had been extremely happy with Jerry's care, with the nursing staff, and with the doctors at St. John's. If we were to go somewhere else, everyone would be a stranger and would not be familiar with his case at all. We decided to stay with St. John's.

Late one evening, the children and I went to F Street and toured the facilities where Jerry would stay until the end of December. He was scheduled for transfer on September 9.

Although Jerry was still in Room 17, and it remained an ICU, it was much more enjoyable to visit with Jerry now. Since he had been taken off the respirator, he could talk with us and tell us what he wanted or needed. He was now worried about us, voicing his concern that we get enough rest and that we eat properly. He talked about eating quite a bit, asking about restaurants around town. He did not get hungry at all, but yet he wanted to eat, desired the taste of food. He wanted to chew something, but he still could not have anything, not even a drink of water. We tried not to talk about food to him, only doing so when he asked about it.

We had been at St. John's a month now and were well acquainted with everyone. The nurses and technicians had become our friends, as had the doctors—especially Dr. Yu. Dr. Yu was born in Hong Kong and is a delightful person. We told jokes to each other, and his vibrant laugh mingled with ours and filled the room, escaping even into the rest of the unit. Jerry's lungs had been severely weakened, and as Dr. Yu was a pulmonary specialist, we saw a lot of him. Our family grew extremely fond of Dr Yu, and we were happy to hear that he would be the one to do Jerry's routine follow-up care when he transferred to rehab.

One day I sat at the nurses station with a doctor, whose name I do not recall, and together we were marveling at the recovery Jerry was having. "Mrs. Buxton, there are at least five things your husband had wrong with him that should have taken him. Any one of them should have killed him." He looked me straight in the eye and said, "He has whipped them all."

Another time, as I sat near the nurse's station, I listened as someone explained to a visitor what was going on in the unit. "And then there is Room 17. You know about our miracle in Room 17." I do not know to whom she spoke, but I know the meaning of the word miracle, and well do I know the man who lay in that room. It is not often that medical people use the word miracle, but we were blessed to hear it often. Once, Kathy told me that Jerry was the most severely injured patient she had ever seen survive. These were happy days; we still had a long way to go, nevertheless, they were happy ones.

I spent the night in the motor home, as I often did now, and was excited as I drove to the hospital early in the morning. Today was Jerry's day of transfer. It would be over; there would be no more ICU visits. I picked up the phone in the waiting room, as I had done so many times, and asked to be admitted. "Come on in, Mrs. Buxton." I walked through the doors, and by the looks on the nurses' faces, immediately I sensed something to be wrong. I rushed to his room and found his face contorted with pain as he struggled for his breath.

"What is wrong?" I demanded, apprehensive, and with the previous feelings of anxiety shrouding me. During the past few hours, he had developed a severe pain in his abdomen and his breathing was becoming increasingly labored. They had begun tests to locate the problem. He was in excruciating pain, and I tried to comfort him.

At about this time, Dr. Yu came in, smiling and friendly, but obviously very concerned. He would do a bronchoscopy to see if he could tell what had developed. I stood by Jerry's head on one side of the bed, Dr. Yu was on the other side, and he told the nurse to set up for the procedure. I was glad he let me stay in the room, but it was quite a challenge to watch. Jerry's gag reflex obviously had returned, as he was gagging violently the whole time. Dr. Yu was yelling. Dr. Yu speaks quite loudly, and he was shouting, "Good. Good. Look at that. Would you look at that?" I was looking, but I really could not tell what was going on, except that I knew that Jerry was gagging, and Dr. Yu was yelling, and I was patting arms and legs and whatever else I could lay my hands on, and maybe I was hyperventilating, and the nurse was flying around doing whatever nurses do in such situations. I could only hope that everything would turn out okay.

"We need a surgical consultation," he concluded. He left the room.

I tried to help Jerry and comfort him, but I could tell he was in extreme distress. I left the room, went out to the nurse's station, and told Eileen that I was worried about his labored breathing. I could tell they all shared my concerns. It wasn't long after reading the report of his latest blood gases, that they told me they must put him back on the respirator. I hated to do it, but I chose to be the one to tell him. He was in such agony, that it actually seemed to be a relief to him. An indication of the extent of his anguish is that to this day he does not remember being intubated again. Dr. Weymer, one of Dr. Yu's colleagues, came to the room to do the procedure. They asked me to leave, and again I sat alone in the waiting room.

18

When they hung the bottles of yellow/green fluid, they told us it was called TPN, and then we learned the initials to be an abbreviation for the words "total parenteral nutrition." TPN is a nutritional solution of glucose, protein hydrolysates, minerals, and vitamins that is used for patients who have a long term situation in which they cannot ingest food in the normal way. One of its side effects is the destruction of the gall bladder.

Dr. Cardan came to Jerry's bed and drew diagrams, giving a brief anatomy lesson, and explaining his surgical plan to remove Jerry's gall bladder. We liked Dr. Cardan; he lived on a small ranch in Ojai, and he had previously told us stories of killing snakes and such—accounts that especially enthralled Chris and Joel. They called him the cowboy doctor.

The conversation around the bed was light, but as I clutched the anatomy drawing, my eyes set on Jerry's form, and I saw anxiety in a pale face that was drawn from pain, with a tube down his throat again. We loved him and prayed with him; then it was time, and they came to take him.

We followed the gurney down the hall, a sad parade now, but not a hopeless or a desolate one. He would make it through this latest setback; he was of a strong will, and indeed, had demonstrated an incredible way of fighting and thrusting for life. He would do it again.

The surgery was an abdominal exploration and all seemed in order except the gall bladder, which contained stones, and had developed gangrene; it was removed. Dr. Cardan also used this opportunity to place a jejunostomy tube, which, too, would be used for Jerry's feedings.[10] He tolerated the procedures well, then was returned to the unit.

At St. John's, ICU surgical patients are taken directly to their rooms after surgery where they are "recovered". It was not long after Dr. Cardan had told us of the surgery's successful conclusion that they let me go in and stand by Jerry's bed. The anesthetic had not worn off, and he was in a deep sleep, again flanked by the multitude of apparatus that seems to accompany the seriously ill person. It seemed to take too long for him to awaken, I thought. Once a wild notion flapped evilly across my mind; what if he should not wake up? "Eileen," I wailed. "Is he sleeping too long?" He was fine, she assured me. Everything looked perfect.

"Mr. Buxton, wake up. Wake up, Mr. Buxton. Your wife is here." Slowly his eyes fluttered, and they opened.

---

[10] *A jejunostomy tube is placed into the jejunum, a portion of the small intestine.*

*In my sleep the pain comes, awakening me as it thrusts and jabs
in my belly. A nurse stands and then a doctor. "Call Shirley. Call
my wife."*

Breath. I need a breath. Why can't I breathe again? Is it the pain?
Why can't they make the pain go away?

Shirley is here, and Dr. Yu. He's yelling now. Why is he yelling at
me? This pain, and I can't breathe. Maybe I can't think, since I can't
breathe. Is this real? Maybe it's only a nightmare.

"It's okay, Jerry. You'll be all right."

Dr. Yu is gagging me and yelling.

Sleep.

A stick again in my throat. It hurts…pain…in my stomach, or
is it my chest?

Surgery? Is that what they said? Surgery again? On what? My
pain?

My breath…I can breathe.

They lift me and move me over. The light changes, I hear doors
open and close, and the bed…the bed rumbles.

"Jerry, hang on, Jerry. You're going to make it."

"Wake up, Mr. Buxton. Wake up. Your surgery's over."

20

We were anxious for Jerry to be off the respirator. We reckoned with the fact that his lungs were dreadfully damaged and weakened, but we had learned too that the longer a patient is connected to a respirator, the harder it is to wean him from it. We encouraged him and encouraged the staff. He progressed well with no major setbacks. On September 13 they set the respirator to blow by, (a respirator setting in which the patient actually does his own breathing) and on the 14th they extubated him. It had been one week since the surgery.

A new transfer date of September 16 was set, and we prepared to leave, gathering his personal items and clearing the walls of cards. We took down the scripture sign and rolled it carefully. We made phone calls to the rest of our family and to our friends.

Jerry was excited and eager to leave, but he had a certain amount of uneasiness. He had voiced apprehension, wishing we could go to Rialto for rehab, instead of staying in Oxnard. Then he would reconsider, and we would talk of how wonderful everyone had been and how they had virtually saved his life. I think too, the thought of leaving the ICU was frightening, as he was yet very sick and helpless. He could do nothing for himself. He still wore the halo brace, and his not being able to swallow caused him to require frequent suctioning.

His limbs lay useless on the bed, capable of very limited movement. IV tubes were still connected to needles in his arms.

It was an emotional time for all of us as we said good-by to the nursing staff, staff who had gone beyond the mere performance of a duty, but instead had entrenched themselves into our hearts, had inched right in to the inner circle of our family. They had become a deep and significant part of our lives, and we would never forget them. We hugged necks and once more voiced our thanks and our extreme gratitude. They had saved Jerry's life, we knew it, and I believe they knew it. The first honor and first credit goes to the Lord Jesus Christ, and without any hesitation we always gave it to Him, and we always will. Life and death are in His hands—only His. He alone had spared Jerry. Yet, God uses people—people's skill, their time, their hands. These people had saved Jerry, and we loved them for it.

Struggle

Congruent with life is struggle. The foolish and uninitiated may anticipate a rich life lived out in ease and comfort, one not allowing the friction of struggle, nor its attendant affliction of anguish; the wise, however, have prepared for the struggle of war and have garbed themselves well. Their minds are steady and fixed. They wear battle gear; they are military tacticians. Corollary to this intelligence is the essential understanding that struggle itself is not a contrary, dissenting force, but that struggle indeed will produce a ripe and glorious life. A discernment of struggle is vital to reason, as few things of great value are attained without struggle.

The fully developed infant, or in less optimum cases, the under developed one, is subjected to essential and lively struggle as the hour of birth approaches. Such forces as never felt before are brought to bear, and although he has no cognition of these pressures, his great skirmish is beginning. Though his mother is involved—for has her body not formed his cave these months—yet his struggle is a separate thing. Her breath has been his life and her food his nourishment. Today, the great separation has begun. Thus, though not cognizant of it, the infant enters the fray. His body is pressed; his heart quickens. He would flail, but he is wedged. He does frown, and then the moment is here. The bones in his head, soft, yet, and flexible, made for this moment, move and slide, so that he may come.

"Hey, it's noisy, and the light is scalding, but I'm cold too. Where is my watery bath, warm and sloshing?" A yelp, a slashed gasp, and he breathes. The struggle ends; yet has it only begun.

Much of our conflict is private, unnoticed by others, internal, even perhaps limited to our own mind. We agonize over philosophy, knowing we must find one. From our resources, our teaching, our life gatherings, we finally form our own; our philosophy for life—the way we will live it. Is it right though? We search the Word of God, ingesting its principles, listening, and then applying them to make sense of our lives. Job was such a man whose end we could predict when we read his beginning, for despite the devastating reports he had received—everything was gone—yet the scripture says, "he worshipped" (Job 1:20).

Worshipped God? you say. Children dead, house destroyed, health gone, naysayers for wife and friends, he had been struck down. He was a wounded man, friction of the highest degree crackling round him, snapping, as does electrical storm on summer evening. Nevertheless, Job had an essential acceptance of his hostile encounter and believed that fresh life would surely come. Though fiercely set upon and entangled, he maintained his integrity before God; he worshipped Him.

Therein is the secret of the ages. We must disregard the stroke of snarling combat, set aside the fearful assaults, and make the ultimate crucial decision: despite these blustering evils, we will worship God, fully and with our whole hearts.

The ultimate struggle is always inward, and there the determination is made: win or lose. Of secondary importance are our bodies, and we have determined that yes, whether glowing with health, or slashed into ribbons, we will rise, even if perhaps we must crawl or be wheeled about in a chair; it is of small actual consequence. Struggle is of the spirit, and is cognitive, soulish, involving the intellect and the anima to much greater degree than is the body so affected. There may lie a body, unable to move; its soul, however, may soar, its spirit intact.

So then, man's greatest struggle is not one of body, of flesh and of corpuscle and bone, but of the psyche and of the soul, for the greatest battleground of all is that of the mind and of the soul. It is in those regions that Satan assaults, walking with booted heel, doing his work, wreaking his havoc. It has been suggested that Jerry's terrible hallucinations could in part have been an attack of Satan, for unquestionably his turf is the human mind. Jerry's body had been snagged, but what of his mind, his psyche, and his soul? Would not it be good to trample him while he was down? Jerry's reaction to morphine and other narcotics spawned a discussion among us of the rampant drug use in America and of the degrading effect of such use.

Who can know if through the drug medium a mind may be opened to morbid and malevolent forces? Is it a gateway for evil? Does Satan avail himself of such opportunity? Does he weasel his way in? Given these premises, granting the mind to be a precious thing, though invisible and not completely defined, should not we carefully guard its gates, scrutinize, and meticulously filter that which would seek access?

The most critical and consequential of Jerry's struggle, and of ours, were mental and spiritual ones, outdistancing even those of the physical, an almost unbelievable statement except to those having crucial spiritual insight and discernment. Although our bodies were mutilated and weary, our capital battles were in our psyche and in our souls, but we fought through them and made the determination that we would overcome. We would cope, we would forgive, Jerry would live, he would eat, and he would walk. However, if he did not, if a particular aspect did not develop as we wished, our internal vigor ordered the decision: we would function as upright human beings, made in the likeness of God, and made a little lower than the angels. We would prevail. Our souls, our psyches, our spirits were in harmony. We had been born to adversity, conceived in sin, and cast out into struggle; now we grappled and agonized as the struggle continued.

I am told that it is only by intense individual struggle that a butterfly comes into being. Metamorphosis takes place: a caterpillar becomes a pupa and is enclosed within a cocoon. The days pass, and now inside the cocoon is a magnificent butterfly, its wings folded and new. It is his time, his moment. He writhes with struggle. Should one observe the cocoon rolling around and jerking with his work, and attempt to bring forth life, the butterfly is doomed. "I will take him from his struggle" are words of defeat and sure death for the butterfly. Should one take into his hand the brown, dry cocoon and begin its unpeeling, the butterfly would be irreparably damaged. His wings are broken and made useless. His developing time of struggle is stolen, and he is destroyed. He flutters and staggers, and dies. Better, instead, that the struggling butterfly presses, heaves and pushes. Finally, there is a crack, a break, the shell crumbles, and from the gloom and into the sparkle comes the magnificent butterfly—a product of ugly brown dryness, of death, of struggle, and of regeneration.

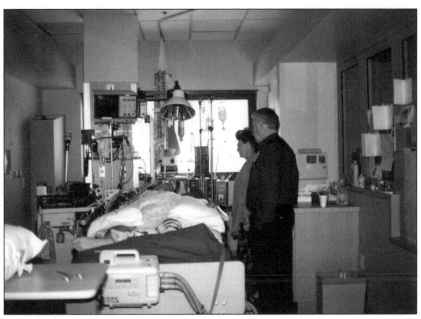

Berl and Lavelta stand by Jerry's bed

Kim helps Jerry stand between the parallel bars

Jerry getting a haircut around his halo

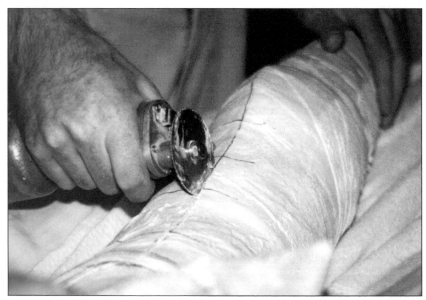

Russ cutting off the leg-brace cast

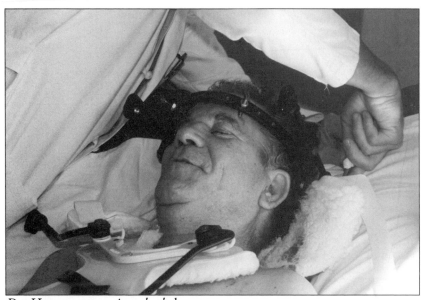

Dr. Herman removing the halo

His sweet nurse Rue helps Jerry into his wheelchair

Lorraine Heter and Jerry

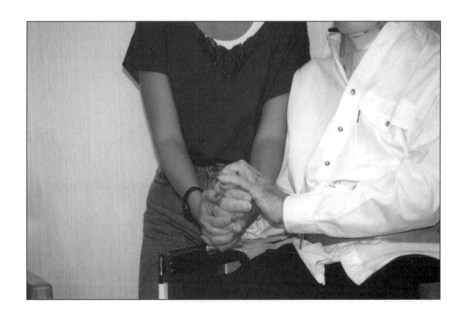

Dr. Yu

Dr. Jaffey

The Healing

"For I will restore health unto thee, and I will heal thee of thy wounds, saith the Lord."

Jeremiah 30:17

21

Jerry had proven himself to be skilled at living and to be a tenacious survivor well before these momentous days. He was born to parents of modest means and was the youngest of twelve children. They lived a simple life in the state of Louisiana. Both his parents died when he was young—his mother when he was four, and his dad, when he was twelve. After that, he had lived with various relatives and with friends. During his senior year of high school, he went to live with his brother Bill, who helped him make the decision to attend Northwestern State College in Natchitoches, LA. He obtained both an academic and a work scholarship, and four years later, he graduated with a Bachelor of Arts degree. He enlisted in the Reserve Officers Training Corp program, and during the summer of 1953, he took his active military training at Fort Bliss, Texas. Many colleges from the southwestern part of the United States sent students for this military training, and Jerry was one of two from that group to receive the Distinguished Military Student Award, a high honor. As a junior, he opened himself to spiritual direction, and it was during these days that he felt called to the ministry. He subsequently resigned his commission as an officer in the Army.

In the fall of 1955, at Apostolic College in Tulsa, Oklahoma, Jerry and I met, and in the spring of 1956, we were married. We moved to California in 1957, where, we have spent most of our lives since then. We did evangelistic work for a few years, and then in 1962 he assumed the pastorate of a church in Garden Grove, California. The church was small and could not financially support us, so Jerry also taught school for eight years. Finally, the church had grown to the point that he could quit teaching, and he became a full-time pastor. We remained there until 1978 when we moved to Rialto to pastor New Life Center.

Jerry had always been active in our church denomination activities and had served on various boards: youth, home missions, Sunday school, and as a presbyter on the Western District Board of the United Pentecostal Church. He was talented with an exceptional baritone voice, and he often had the opportunity to lead worship services in both small and very large meetings.

Now again, he had proved his mettle and had survived when it seemed impossible. The staff lifted him onto a gurney and rolled him out of the ICU. They trekked down the halls and into the ambulance. The rehabilitation unit was a few blocks away, and I followed the ambulance in my car, then stood close as they moved him through the doors and into the new facility.

His large room was a private one close to the entrance and to the nurses' station, and with a window that looked onto F Street. We set about making the room pleasant, pasting up the scripture sign and the cards he had received. The nurses seemed disconcerted when he arrived, as though he had come sooner than they had expected. It was my impression that they felt him to be sicker than they expected. We learned it to be exceptional for a patient to transfer directly from the ICU. Instead, the patient usually moved onto a regular nursing floor, then went over to rehab. However, the doctors had deemed him ready to begin his physical therapy, and we were eager for him to start.

Jerry's mood was multi-faceted. He recognized his life to have been inexorably altered and realized that the weeks and months ahead would be filled with extreme challenges as he worked through the rehabilitation processes. He knew that any expectation he had for full recovery was unrealistic, that is, according to medical information and prognoses. That knowledge caused him grief and a certain amount of depression. His faith, however, was intact. His wounded body housed an unfettered spirit that had never given to gauzy bandages, nor had it been imprisoned within plaster cast, starkly white and rigid. That accident had bound and stricken his body to the bed one could not deny; contravening, though, was that his essence was free—free not only to be, but also to act. Thus, he shifted himself from the realm of incapacitated patient-prisoner who has no hope to that of a grasping survivor who would call on his every resource to effect his recovery. One of his colleagues, Robert Bayer, spoke well to Jerry: "I know you will make it; you will recover because of your indomitable will."

In addition, truly he was a man of God, who during his adult years had lived his life in accordance with the Bible, looking there for direction. His life and that of his family were centered on the things of God. He knew God. He had walked with Him for many years; God was real and personal to him and Jerry had forged a loving relationship with Him. He would lean on divine fellowship and Godly guidance. He was expecting a miracle, and he would not quit.

His room had an extra bed in it, and usually I spent the night there. I became quite involved in his care and rapidly acquainted myself with the personnel in this new facility. Each morning I went to our motor home where I dressed for the day and then returned, remaining there for most of the day. We talked, I assisted with much of his nursing needs, and I observed many of his therapy sessions. I only left to eat meals and to take care of business.

It was truly teamwork at the rehab center and myriad disciplines were involved, each group drawing from their educational background and offering expertise and aid in helping the patients to recover. Dr. Judy was in complete charge of the rehabilitation hospital, and we communicated with him frequently. Dr. Yu came to see

Jerry daily, assuming the position of his primary care doctor who called in specialists as such need arose. The hospital nurses were the ones responsible for his primary care, dispensing medications, bathing him, and scheduling his lab work and X-rays at the main hospital, seeing to his day to day care. It so happened that many of the nurse's aids were Filipino, and they were exceptionally sweet. He had wonderful nurses.

Although others worked with him during his stint there, Kim was his primary physical therapist; she was blond and tiny but as was the case with all the therapists, she was quite strong. The focus of the Physical Therapy Department is the evaluation and treatment of bodily dysfunction that particularly relates to mobility, muscle strength, and balance in sitting and standing. It also includes breathing and coughing assessments. Many months later, Kim told us that after reading of Jerry's condition and after meeting him, she had felt overwhelmed, and considered at length the rehabilitation of one so injured. Occupational Therapy is involved with the teaching of daily living skills. They often design and teach the use of appliances that will assist the patient in developing these abilities. Jackie was Jerry's primary OT therapist. Jerry was involved in speech and language activities because of his swallowing problem, and in addition, he spent time in Recreational Therapy. A social worker, a chaplain, and a psychologist were also assigned to him.

It was evident from the beginning that our family would also be included in his work, sometimes only as observers, but later as assistants. Jerry became extremely close to these wonderful people, as did I, and we think of them as dear friends.

Leaders from each discipline examined Jerry thoroughly and after evaluating him, they recorded their findings. Then they charted their individual discharge goals on a form called Functional Independence Measure; as before, the prognoses were poor. Their expectations: at his time of discharge Jerry would not be mobile, nor in any physical way be completely independent. They did not tell us these things at the time, although I believe they were honest with us; actually, they told us there was no way to know the degree of Jerry's recovery. They held out hope, a starry thing to which we stretched. An illuminating point is that on this same chart his mental potential was ascribed a seven, the highest possible rating. Even at this early stage of his recovery, it was obvious that despite his severe brain injuries, his cognitive faculties were intact. A tender mercy. To this moment, we utter praise.

Jerry's feeling of helplessness was somewhat alleviated by the incremental development of some small independent movement of his limbs and by the slow return of sensory perceptions throughout his body. Once as he was alone in the room, his left arm jerked up and landed on his chest. Startled, he rolled his eyes downward and said, "Hello there!" Although he tried, he could not move his arm off his chest, but finally it slid down onto the bed. Jerry excitedly told Steve about it that afternoon, and Steve wanted to see him move his arm, but he was not able to do it again. After he had been in rehab a couple of weeks, the staff installed a magic touch call light system that he was able to use with his left hand.

Daily, he improved. He was a cooperative patient, and he worked hard, having at least two therapy sessions every weekday. When it was time for him to go to therapy, it took three people to transfer him to the wheelchair, then to the mat, or back in his bed, but he was able to sit up for an hour and a half now. The doctors told us that Jerry's left knee was severely damaged and that eventually he must have it replaced. In the meantime, its instability was a hindrance to his rehab activities, so they called in Russ Eldeb for an orthotic consultation, resulting in the decision to fabricate a Bledsoe hinged brace. Russ was burly and likable, and Jerry would see him frequently as his equipment and braces were designed. The next day, Russ went to Jerry's bed to form a cast, from which he would make the brace. He mixed up a concoction and began work on Jerry's leg. He wrapped the limb with what looked to be gauze and plaster, then let it do its work of forming the mold. The chemicals created heat that was uncomfortably hot, and Jerry yelped. He seemed relieved when Russ cut the whole thing off. Russ went out the door with what appeared to be Jerry's leg tucked under his arm.

Jerry tired easily, cried frequently, and slept poorly. "Depression and anxiety have become more apparent as the patient and his wife have been confronting the reality of their situation" is a direct quote from the medical chart dated September 29. It was true. He tried to have faith and to be positive and to believe, as did I, but sometimes it threatened to overwhelm him and to overwhelm me.

Russ brought the Bledsoe, a heavy metal brace hinged at the knee. He put it on Jerry's leg, and he showed me how to strap it on. Jerry had developed a little strength in his left arm, and one day they set him in an electric wheel chair with a left arm drive, but he couldn't quite maneuver it. Someone from OT came down and said they would fabricate a device to help him operate the switches. The therapists taught me how to do gentle range of motion exercises for his right hand. "We will try to give you food," they said one day, and they conducted a feeding evaluation beside his bedside. He choked, and the therapists recommended a videofluoroscopy swallow evaluation. Until then, though, he must ingest no food or drink. They began feedings through his J-tube, and he tolerated that well.

He saw the nurse come with a sign, and he wondered what it said. Although he could not move his head because of the halo brace, Jerry had become adept at extreme movement of his eyes. As the nurse moved about the room and then mounted the sign over his bed, he strained intensely to be able to read it: HOW TO CARE FOR THE QUADRIPLEGIC. She seemed not to know that he had read the sign, and she left the room.

He was stunned. Fear sprang at him, its deadly claws squeezing his tortured lungs and mutilated brain, as does jungle cat that at once pounces, snarling her mastery. He was alone in the room, and he sank; the aloneness being a ghastly instrument of discouragement. A quadriplegic? Not I—surely not. He reckoned with himself, acknowledging himself paralyzed and virtually helpless. Both arms and both legs were affected, so he conceded that by strict definition the sign was true. His working through the definition though did nothing to relieve him of the tormenting terror that now piled on him. His room became a dungeon, black questions swirling. Was this truly to be his lot?…How would he minister?…Who would tend his family?…Was it over?…Was life over for him?

I came into his room later in the day, and immediately I glimpsed the sign. I saw too, that Jerry was in a hole of fear and discouragement. I bent over, and twisting my mouth around the rods of the halo brace, I kissed his troubled face. He was terrified—a vulnerable child. We talked, both of us trying to be strong and both of us saying the words we thought to be the right ones. A nurse came in and handed me a white binder. With trembling hands, I took the slick notebook, and with wary eyes, I read its title: SPINAL CORD INJURY—Patient/Family Education Handbook. Her manner was gentle as she turned the pages with me.

During the night, as one of the aids tended him, Jerry began to cry, frustrated tears of helpless sorrow and of disappointment. He shook with fear. She put down her charts, and seating herself on his bed, she took up a helpless hand. Softly, she spoke words of hope and of healing. With a tissue, she dried his eyes. She rubbed him, and patted him, and soon he was calmed. Before he slept though… was he not a preacher…and she was having these problems…and what did he think…and did he have knowledge of such situation?….Before he slept, the roles had reversed: the preacher was again the minister, and the young woman a suppliant who wiped her own tears of sorrow.

22

Jerry refused to stay depressed, and he refused to identify himself as a quadriplegic, at least he would not admit to being a long-term quadriplegic—a real, genuine quadriplegic. Maybe a recovering quadriplegic, or a temporary one; perhaps he could handle that. That, though, was his limit. He would accept no more. He would whip this. He would walk again.

Would he preach, though? His voice problem troubled him; he considered the great effort of preaching, and he wondered if he would be able to go to a pulpit again and deliver a fiery Pentecostal sermon. He vividly recalled the story of his colleague Alan Oggs who, when recovering from heart surgery, had suffered the same fears and concerns. "Did they take my preacher?" Alan Oggs wondered, and once when his room was empty of nurses and visitors he "held forth," dredging up one of his sermons and hurling the words around the sterile room. It still worked, he decided. His preacher was yet there. Now the question was Jerry's. Could he do it? Did he have the faculties, and would he have the strength? It was a troubling concern and one that lasted many days.

Medical notes—October 6: "He is highly motivated to participate in the rehab program. He receives a tremendous amount of support from family and friends and uses his religious beliefs and faith as a coping resource…a family conference emphasized how well he was progressing."

Jerry's lung capacity had increased. He could turn the wheelchair on and off and could sit in it for two hours. The therapists taught me to give him pressure reliefs, in which every thirty minutes I would lift him slightly from the chair then lower him again. It now required less effort to transfer him from the bed to the chair than before. He could sit on the mat, his hands in his lap, for up to ten minutes. He learned how to recover himself from falling. In OT, they rigged an overhead sling so that he could assist in brushing his teeth.

Medical notes—October 13: "The patient continues to make steady improvements overall. He was highly disappointed to recently learn that he had a paralyzed vocal cord which interferes with his vocal quality and may impact on his future as a pastor."

OT therapy continued to focus on his oral hygiene abilities. He used the dorsal wrist orthosis and held a uniquely formatted toothbrush. As a therapist guided his elbow, he was able to bring his hand to his mouth.

Medical notes—October 20: "Patient is continent of bowel and bladder on demand…" A tender mercy. To this moment, we utter praise.

In the therapy room they strapped Jerry down flat, then stood by as the mat slanted and raised, finally tilted to such degree that he stood upright. His heart was a jackhammer and the room blazed and spun wildly. Then they lowered him and checked his pulse and his blood pressure. "How do you feel?"

"I feel wonderful!" He grinned. Soon he could brush his teeth without the dorsal wrist splint by still using the built-up handled toothbrush, and with one of us guiding his elbow and forearm as he reached upward.

Jerry was not comfortable with the Bledsoe brace, nor were the therapists pleased with it, so Russ came in and made adjustments that he hoped would increase the lateral stability in Jerry's left leg. There was talk of the standing frame.

During the week of October 20, I walked beside him as Jerry powered his wheelchair down the hall for another therapy session. The therapists directed him to the standing frame. The standing frame has an apparatus on which the patient sits with belts securely strapping him in. Jerry was exhilarated as he sat there, his face radiant and animated. He was ready for this: I had my camera. A therapist stood on either side of him and pushed a button that elevated the seat and changed its configuration. Slowly, it lifted him so that he stood upright with his weight on both feet. I snapped pictures of him and of his blood pressure reading, which was perfect; he yelled, and every person in the room, whether visitor, patient, or medical staff, grinned and cheered. Within days, he could stand for ten minutes at a time.

In Recreational Therapy, he selected a ceramic cup to paint. Jerry did that—he, the man proud of his masculine nature and not a whit inclined toward the arts or the crafts, except that his singing had been as an angel. We snickered together, as with reluctant hands made capable only by the close help of his therapist, he daubed on the paint and then sent the chalice for firing. It was to be a gift to his good friend Sam but when we left in December we had misplaced it, and we never saw the vessel again. A shame—it was a beauty.

We had a chaplain assigned to us, and although it was obvious that we were surrounded by spiritual support, we appreciated his coming by, and he and Jerry had some interesting discussions. "After you leave here, why don't you come back and make rounds with me?" the chaplain said one day. Jerry thought he would like that and agreed to do so.

Each Friday afternoon the happy roundup took place. Every patient was encouraged to meet in the recreation room for group therapy, and as the meeting time neared, the halls filled with patients heading that way. Dr. Jaffey, a clinical psychologist, was in charge, and often she wheeled patients in for the session herself. Any family members were welcome, and we were encouraged to participate, both with our attendance and with our verbal contributions. These were interesting and helpful sessions that Jerry and I both came to anticipate. They lasted about an hour and a half. Dr. Jaffey usually had a subject to discuss, but she was always open to anything that another person needed to talk about. She brought refreshments, and we threw simple parties for a patient who was to be discharged or who had made some special progress. She asked someone from the group to conclude each session with a closing word; often it was a prayer. At first Jerry was so sick and his speaking ability so poor that he was quiet and did not participate much. However, Dr. Jaffey drew everyone into the conversation, and soon he was deeply involved in all the discussions, often concluding the afternoon's activities with prayer.

Our friends continued to visit Jerry, so many that at one point his nurses thought to restrict them to the weekends so that he would have the energy he needed for his therapy sessions. We had mixed feelings about that as we knew he needed time to rest and sleep, and yet we felt his emotional and spiritual needs to be so great that he also needed his friends and colleagues. We tried to balance it. One afternoon, as his room resounded with laughter, Dr. Jaffey peered in the doorway. "What is going on in here? You people are always laughing." Dr. Jaffey was young and vibrant, and we loved her. She had black hair and snappy dark eyes.

I told her that we laughed because we had joy, the kind of joy that comes from the Holy Ghost. It springs from a deep and personal relationship with God and is not dependent on circumstances, we told her. We spoke further of joy and of faith, and we invited her to a Pentecostal church service. We explained in detail the spontaneous and unique worship she would experience. She was Jewish, she told us, and at one point in her life she had consulted with her rabbi about that very subject. "I want joy," she had told him.

We all want joy, whether Jew or Gentile, we had concluded as we spoke that day. It was appropriate to have such discussion and to take it a step further as we reckoned with there being a distinct difference between joy and happiness. None of us was happy with Jerry's being in this terrible situation, but our joy was undiminished, predicated on internal circumstances that neither injury or disease could mutilate or injure. We cultivated joy, flinging it generously around the room and up and down the halls. It was contagious, and it was healing.

Several times, Rick Manzer had gone to the acute hospital to inquire after Jerry and me. One day he called the rehab center saying he wanted his family to visit Jerry. He brought them, leading his children close to the bed. We were complete strangers when we met on the street, but now we had formed a unique bond. Rick recognized that he had been part of a developing miracle. "Touch my children," he said to Jerry. Jerry did so and prayed for them, taking care to explain that there was nothing special in his touch. "The touch of God is what you need," Jerry told him.

It was now November, and during the first week of the month, exciting things happened. For one, the therapists took away Jerry's electric wheel chair, teasing him and saying he was getting too wild with it. His brother and his sister-in-law, Herb and Edna, came to visit, and when they had driven onto the parking lot, something strange-looking wheeled around making feeble motions with his arms and directing them into a parking space. The impish face that peered at them as they parked was Jerry's, gleeful and bright. Now he had a manual wheelchair, and he could propel it 30 feet. The therapists timed him as he roared up and down the halls. He loved it.

They took him to the parallel bars, and he stood; he stood for three minutes, and for four, then for ten minutes. He lifted a foot, and he stepped forward. Once Jerry looked down at Kim as she worked with him and asked, "Kim, do you think I will ever walk again?"

She considered before she answered, averting her face, then she looked at him and spoke: "If anyone with injuries like yours will ever walk, it will be you."

He loved Kim.

In OT, he shaved a portion of his face. He held a cup with his left hand. He brushed his teeth. He was trundled down the hall in his wheelchair, I trundling beside him. He had his first shower since

August. He was ecstatic. His left grip strength had increased from zero to ten pounds, his right from zero to eight/ten pounds.

Russ came back and measured him for a brace for his right leg. He fabricated a plaster form and walked out the front door, again carrying Jerry's leg.

During the second week of November, Jerry went by ambulance to the main hospital where technicians took extensive X-rays of his neck. The reports showed excellent healing of his fracture; the halo brace could come off! Dr. Herman came to his bed to remove it, and Jerry's room was full of people, our family and friends and as many of the nursing and therapy staff as could squeeze in. It was a party. Rather quickly, the removal was complete, the heavy vest and its steel rods gone, along with the pins in his head. He had been in the halo brace for three months. Dr. Herman placed a stiff cervical collar on his neck that he would wear for a few days, and then for a few weeks, he would wear a soft brace. His neck was weak because of the long immobilization, and his muscles needed support while they regained their strength. During group therapy, we had a halo removal celebration. We ate cake and beamed at Jerry.

However, Jerry himself could not eat cake or anything else, and it was time for doctors to further evaluate his swallowing difficulty. Again, I followed the ambulance and went with him to the radiology department. Dr. Berrett thoroughly explained what they would be doing and showed me where to stand so that I could watch during the actual testing. Jerry attempted to swallow thickened liquids, pureed food, and a thin liquid. It was intriguing to watch, as on the screen I could see the food moving down his throat. He had some problems swallowing the thick liquids and the pureed foods, but compensatory strategies in which they instructed him helped clear the pooling and the residue. I saw also that he immediately aspirated the thin liquids, although he did not cough. They did not continue with further testing, and when Jerry learned the results, he was very disappointed.

However, in spite of the test results, they began feeding him very small amounts of food, carefully observing him at all times. They taught him compensatory strategies, which he must observe with every spoonful of thickened liquids, and the occasionally pureed food he could try:

1. Do a dry swallow
2. Flex his head forward and to the left
3. Swallow the food
4. Turn his head left
5. Cough
6. Do a dry swallow

Jerry became adept at following these procedures, and the simple food tasted so delicious that he did not complain, and at last, we laughed about it.

Faith was a rehab patient who had suffered a stroke, and she also had to perform compensatory maneuvers when she ate. After a few days of eating privately in his room where a therapist closely observed him, Jerry went to join Faith in a private dining room. There they ate together. Her maneuvers were different from his, and since we all had a good sense of humor we chortled at the peculiar noises and funny faces they made as each of them extended and flexed and snorted. However, they did swallow, and they did not choke.

Jerry could not consume enough food for his needs so they continued with his J-tube feedings. His nurses taught me the procedure and I often carried out his feeding process.

Though she had communicated frequently with us, Jerry had not personally talked with Lorraine Heter, the young lady who had revived him on Oxnard Blvd. We had talked by telephone, and she had written a letter that told of her episode with her dying father, saying also that the experience of pulling back Jerry from death had obliterated the guilt she had felt over not saving her father. Now, she had called again and would come to visit him. Many of our family and friends would be there, and someone had notified the *Los Angeles Times* who would send a reporter. We gathered in the recreation room. Jerry sat stiffly, his skull held rigid by the stiff collar that circled his neck. He was eager and apprehensive. We watched him as she walked through the door. She was tall and beautiful, and she came with a friend. She stood in the doorway, then her eyes roved, and she saw him. Their eyes met. She walked to him and bent over his body. They wept.

The reporter interviewed the two and snapped pictures. Then it was our turn and we tried to say thanks—thanks to a beautiful young woman who had saved our loved one from death.

Often now, we think of her and call her name. We remember.

23

Jerry continued to make phenomenal progress in all areas. The physical therapists had begun gentle cervical range of motion activities, and for a period of as long as three hours, he had been out of his neck brace. His wheelchair transfers were smoother, and he required only one person to help. With assistance, he could transition from sit to stand in the parallel bars, and he could walk 15 feet, although his right leg brace bothered him. Russ and the therapists were trying to correct the problem. He could propel his wheelchair 120 feet in two and one-half minutes. He could now brush his teeth, his elbow on the table for support, and wash his own hands and face, although he still could not comb his hair. He could not dress his lower body, but with some assistance and by using a buttonhook holder, he was able to button his shirts.

The staff wanted us in for a family training session, so on November 17 Andrew, Steve, and I met with the therapists to prepare for Jerry's first pass. He would be home for Thanksgiving—a two-day visit. It was a blessing that we had been able to stay close by him and that we had participated in many therapy sessions during the previous months. We had talked at great length with the doctors, the therapists, and the nurses. We had studied medical terms and had asked many questions. We knew how to dispense his medication, how to dress him, and how to feed him through his J-tube. Frequently, we had assisted with bedside transfers. We had suctioned him and bathed him; we had tended him in every way. The excellent staff professionally walked us through the training. We each believed ourselves to be competent, and we felt comfortable with taking him home. We were ready.

Ready? Excited? Eager? Our excitement and eagerness could have been as nothing compared to those of Jerry himself, who had long anticipated this day, this day of release. Homebound! Home for the holidays!

Worse than preparing to travel with a baby was the gathering of his paraphernalia, clothes, medication, and special food—and the subsequent loading into the car. Finally though, we had shoved it in; the car was at the entrance, its doors wide, and with great fanfare, we rolled him out. He performed a splendid transfer, someone buckled him in, folded the wheelchair and stuck it in with the other things, and we were gone.

As we neared the north portion of Rialto and made the last familiar turns, an emotional quietness came over us, and from the edge of our eyes, we watched to see his reaction at the first sight of home. The brace hindered moving his neck, but ever so slowly, he turned and gazed. Nearly four months before, he had powered down this street, capable and strong, having no whisper of the way he would return.

One of the neighbors hurried over for a few words, and then we rolled him inside. It was a breathless moment, and we paused in the entryway. It was truly with thanksgiving and with gratitude that he took it in, his own home and his family, so dear and so precious to him. It had been a tiring day for him and after talking for awhile, we put him to nap. "What a wonderful bed this is," he said.

The doctors thought Jerry's risk of choking was so great that he should not eat while he was away from the hospital. Therefore, his only food while at home would be his tube feedings. Consequently, I decided not to cook a Thanksgiving dinner. Throughout the months when Jerry could not eat, we had been thoughtful of his feelings, and we usually did not take food into his room. Now, I surely did not want him to smell roasting turkey and spicy pumpkin pies when he could not eat any of it. We would not cook. I had discussed it with the children, and we had agreed that it is not the food and drink that make a holiday. Rather, it is the gathering of friends and family, and the social and spiritual dynamics that create a holiday and that ring in a celebration. We formed a simple plan. From time to time throughout the day, small groups of us would drive to Carrows, a coffee shop that stood a few blocks away. We would eat our dinner there.

We built a fire in the family room, and when Jerry awoke, we wheeled him into the middle of us. We played games at the table and sneaked into the kitchen to eat pies that friends had brought. We talked of the hospital and of the accident, of the past and of the future. We were thankful, truly we were. It was our best Thanksgiving ever.

On Thanksgiving night, Jerry slept, as did I; our bodies were each warm to the other.

Through the years, it had developed into a ritual, our drinking coffee and reading the paper early each morning. We had missed it these last months, and though Jerry could not participate fully this Friday morning, I did my part, sharing the paper with him and drinking enough coffee for both of us. However, he would not be left out, and at the scheduled times, I opened a can of liquid food and conducted it into his system. Someone built a fire and the rest of us ate bowls of cereal in the kitchen; it was a wonderful morning. The boys and I spent a fair amount of time assessing needed structural changes, so that Jerry would be able to maneuver safely when he came home permanently. We would get a carpenter to alter the shower so that Jerry could easily transfer from his wheelchair onto the shower bench. Perhaps we would order a ramp for the front entrance.

By early evening, we were back in Oxnard, reporting a delightful and successful two-day home visit.

"Mr. Buxton, how would you like to visit your friends in the ICU?" Kim asked him one day. Someone had told us that patients seldom return to visit the ICU staff, and this was definitely something Jerry wanted to do.

Kim set up the visit. We drove Jerry over in our car, and she met us there, along with many of our friends and family. It was all so familiar to us but strange to Jerry, and as we went through the entrance, down the halls, and up the elevator, we explained everything. We had showed him the rooms where we waited the night of his surgeries, and now we wheeled him into the ICU reception room. One of us picked up the telephone and announced that he had arrived. "Come in," the clerk said.

They were expecting him, and the nurses swarmed around his wheelchair. Kathy had the day off, and she had come in just for this visit, bringing her grandchildren with her. She bent low over him, her hair mingling with his. I tried not to, but I could not help myself: I cried, as did others.

Kim stood close by. Then she spoke: "Would you like to see Mr. Buxton walk?" They pushed his chair directly before the door of Room 17. He prepared himself, both physically and emotionally. Facing the door, and looking directly onto the bed where he had lain, he rose and stood. He walked.

24

Our financial situation was grievous, causing me extensive distress and worry. I spoke little of this to Jerry for I did not want to add to his burdens; his platter was well filled. I, though, was near a panic every time I thought of our finances, which was every day. Nothing seemed to be working out, everything seemed complicated, and I really did not know what to do. I spoke with friends and my family, and they were supportive, but there was not much to say, and I knew it was up to me to resolve this. I had to get something done. I made every effort to get assistance from Medi-Cal; they told me to take everything out of Jerry's name. It was difficult to do that.

Shortly after moving to rehab, I located a notary public in a small shopping center and asked if he would go to Jerry's room and notarize a document. He was not friendly, and it was evident that he truly did not want to do it, but he agreed to meet me there. When he arrived, he asked for Jerry's identification. Identification? We had none. I long had taken his wallet to the motor home, and I had nothing. Why hadn't I thought of needing identification? The man stood there and looked at me. I tried to talk him into doing the deed, but he would not. The nurses and the doctors could surely identify him, but no, that was not official. He must see documentation. He left. (I actually do understand the need for documentation of a person's identity and realize that, no doubt, the gentleman's decision followed routine and acceptable business practices.)

Everything seemed that way. Someone would point to a promising corner and each one I turned dissolved into sheer confusion. It was obvious Jerry would need extensive time off from preaching, and that perhaps he would never even preach again. I needed tax strategy advice. Someone recommended an attorney who had expertise in such affairs, and Steve and I made an appointment with him. His office was magnificent, located in a splendid high rise in LaJolla. We laid out the situation, asking for advice, and he indicated that he could help. We never heard from him again, despite calling his office repeatedly.

The personnel at St. John's, though, were tremendous, and although they actually could do nothing for me at the time, they tried, and were friendly and supportive. Jackie, the social worker at rehab, often inquired about our situation.

Finally, I had everything finished for the Medi-Cal application. I submitted the papers, and rather quickly, someone, somewhere, stamped the papers and returned them: DENIED.

More promising was that Jerry would qualify for Social Security disability benefits, and although these funds would not apply to his current medical bills, it was encouraging that in a few months he would receive this income. I obtained a large packet of papers; I plowed my way through and submitted them.

The Victims of Violent Crime had heard of our plight and two gentlemen came to the rehab conference room to meet with me. They said that Jerry was eligible for their help because the driver of the other car had been drunk. Although I truly did appreciate their proposal, the amount they had to disperse was quite small, and I might need to repay it. However, I was grasping, and when they handed me a large packet of application papers, I plowed through those too. They also told me that they had a motorized scooter they wished to donate to Jerry. We bought a new battery, and later in the month took the scooter home with us.

25

Recreational Therapy was in charge of seasonal decorations, and now that it was December, they worked to transform the simple halls and meeting rooms into festive places of cheer. We hung decorations in Jerry's room, and people began sending Christmas cards. Dr. Judy told us that Jerry's scheduled date for release was December 23, and after that, he would need several months of outpatient therapy. On December 1, we had a lengthy session during which we ordered equipment he would take home, including a wheelchair, a walker, a shower bench, a slide board to assist in his transfers, and one other marvelous and indispensable bathroom item.

The staff timed him in the hall, and now he could zoom 300 feet in three and one-half minutes. He roared by. He could walk 25 feet with a front-wheeled walker. With help, he could comb his hair. He manipulated building blocks and nesting cups; he stacked things, and he felt of items in his hand and tried to identify them. "Is it a pin? Does this feel sharp? Dull? How about this?" He scooted on mats; he tried to roll over, but he could not. He painted his cup. OT planned shopping trips, and did he wish to go? and no, he did not. The accident, to be sure, had altered him in many ways, but it is significant that his outlook on shopping was not so affected.

He also had become the unofficial resident chaplain, the lifter of heads, the healer. He traveled the halls dispensing joy, joking, and teasing. His room was down the hall now, and at times, roommates came. If they were despondent, he cheered them. If their families were flagging, he propped them. He spoke scripture, recommended prayer, and pointed with grace and gratitude to his own recovery. The friend next door was struggling with the changes his broken neck had brought. Jerry wheeled into his room, and together they talked of their blessings, of their families, and of ways they would cope, of methods they would use to survive. A lady wearing a halo brace came into the unit, weepy. "Please go speak with her," Dr. Jaffey said to Jerry. Jerry thundered to her in his green rolling chair.

Dr. Yu saw Jerry daily, and they had become friends; indeed, he had become a family friend. Although from divergent backgrounds and unlike disciplines, they had drawn resolutely together. Their link was common purpose: Jerry's healing. A brotherhood had formed, a camaraderie. It is hard to think that anyone who had seen the extent of Jerry's injuries and his subsequent recovery would be unwilling to apply the word miracle. Dr. Yu had been with Jerry since the beginning hours of his torture, and he appeared to recognize that this situation was singular and of notable import. "I would like to bring Mary Kay and my son to visit with you, Gerald," he said one day. So, he brought them, his sweet wife and Daniel, who played on the floor. Daniel was two years old, and he insisted on emptying the wastebasket repeatedly. "I think he will be a trashman," Dr. Yu laughed. "The trash can is his favorite toy."

"Gerald, you are the most remarkable man I have ever met during my 18 years of practice," Dr. Yu said one Sunday morning as he stood over his bed.

Remarkable? Jerry thought. How can I be remarkable? Stretched out here as a mummy, not able to get up and down by myself. Remarkable? Nevertheless, he quickly ascertained the scope of Dr. Yu's remarks, and he spoke aloud: "Dr. Yu, there is nothing remarkable about me. It is God who is remarkable."

They spoke for a long time that Sunday morning. They talked of Jerry's accident and of his healing. Jerry commended the doctors for their splendid care and for their expertise. They spoke of God and of miracles. They discussed the Bible and what it means, and when Dr. Yu said he did not know how to read the Bible, Jerry teased him and said he would gladly interpret scripture for him. They spoke of goals and of dreams. They uttered phrases of life, both of the physical and the eternal.

Once on another occasion, Jerry asked: "Dr. Yu, does the spinal cord ever repair itself?"

"No, we have no record of the spinal cord itself ever regenerating." Then he looked intently at Jerry and continued. "But in your case—your cord could have been severed and your God would have grown you another."

The weekends at rehab had a different feel to them. There were no active therapy sessions, nor scheduled trips to labs or X-ray units, and except for the pleasant buzz of visitors who came more often on weekends, it was quieter. Each Sunday, I left early in the morning for my Rialto church visit and returned in the late afternoon. It could be a lonesome day for Jerry, but preachers and their families ministered to him then, as at other times. Often Larry Alred, a local pastor, brought his wife, Jessie, for a lengthy afternoon visit with Jerry, and sometimes they gathered around the recreation room piano and sang simple hymns. The families of Fred Davis and Kenneth Fields also visited frequently.

Once when Jerry sat on a mat in the physical therapy gym, a young man from an Oxnard church strode firmly into the room. He wore a tuxedo, and in his case, he carried an electric bass guitar. He announced Jerry to be the object of his concert, but others were welcome to listen. He seated himself and played lilting classical music. We never knew if he had obtained permission, or if he had just pressed in, but his performance seemed to be acceptable, and the music was beautiful. We judged it a precious tribute: tribute to an aging, injured pastor from a vibrant, young Christian.

Jerry's swallowing skills had improved so that the staff discontinued supervised feeding sessions, and when his December 9 videofluoroscopy was analyzed, they advanced him to a regular diet. "Just be careful," the nurse told him. Someone gave him a coupon for In-N-Out, in Jerry's estimation, the world's finest hamburger place. We obtained a pass, and as we prepared to leave one afternoon, Larry Booker came into the room.

"This treat will be on me," he said when he heard of the hamburger trip. Larry Booker wheeled Jerry in at the restaurant, and returning from the counter, he set down a tray of delicious greasy hamburgers with mounds of scorching french-fries. It was a feast. Jerry's face radiated, and no doubt, our own faces reflected his joy.

An evening pass was an opportunity for our family to take Jerry to a restaurant where we would eat a fine meal. We chose one that overlooked the sea, and that was quiet with few other people dining. Our table was circular and set against a large window. Lights glittered against the dark night, and beside us, a tall Christmas tree glowed. When the food came, it was Jerry, who, as we bowed our heads began to say the blessing. Could there be voice to speak without rending at such a moment? Did we not feel a teary sting behind our burning eyes? Then finally, our voices mingled with his as we lifted thanks for the food—and for the eating.

Passes were easy to obtain now, for both Jerry and I needed to have practical experience before his discharge. We attended Christmas dramas at two local churches. Faith wanted to go too, and as she had been discharged by then, we drove by her house to get her. We were a sight as we parked at the church. I was the only able-bodied one of our trio, and as I struggled to lift the wheelchair out of the trunk, making more commotion than should have been necessary due to my distressing lack of mechanical ability, she was tortuously trying to escape from the car's interior. Finally she and her walker were out, and she was feebly trying to help me get Jerry free when an usher saw us and came over to help. We laughed at ourselves: it was easier that way, and besides, she and Jerry had snorted and lurched together for a long time.

One evening, a group of us put jackets on our charges and wheeled them out for a three-block F Street jaunt. The air was cold and magnificent. Stately houses, old and tall, sat far back on their lawns, mixed in with white wooden cottages. Sometimes we would see unit numbers stamped on the doors, and we knew that someone had split a fine place into apartments. That lovely brick one was a nunnery, someone said. Jerry and I talked a little as we strolled along, the essence of the holiday surely not lost on us. Christmas lights blinked and the scent of rapture was upon us.

Carolers came into the facility and sang through the halls. We traveled again to Rialto and gathered with our church family for our annual Christmas banquet. Some saw Jerry for the first time since August. Those few hours were golden and passionate ones.

26

Now Jerry could propel his wheelchair 400 feet in four minutes, and with a walker and one person to help, he could ambulate 75 feet in four to five minutes. He could button his shirt without using any device, but he still needed help with dressing his lower body. Although Russ had made adjustments, he was never comfortable with the right leg brace. Finally, he said he did not want to wear it, and he discarded it.

Medical notes—December 15: "Mr. Buxton continues to make incredible gains, and both he and his family have initiated all possible community agency referrals for additional assistance."

During the last weeks we were in Oxnard, some remarkable things occurred. The first involved Dr. Yu.

I was sitting by Jerry's bed when Dr. Yu came in to have a serious talk with us. It was about money—the money we owed the hospital and the money we owed the doctors. We had paid nothing, and I felt my face grow hot with embarrassment at the thought. "I have a suggestion," he said. He took paper and pen from his pocket and asked: "How many doctors do you owe? How **much** do you owe them?"

I was not sure, and Jerry surely did not know, and when I said that, Dr. Yu told me he needed a list of the doctors, along with the amount we owed each one. There were around twenty groups of doctors, but I could easily devise a statement, for in the motor home I had all the bills.

He went right on talking. "Let me tell you what I am going to do." He looked first at Jerry, then at me. "I am going to the financial office of St. John's and ask them to forgive you of your entire debt." We gawked at him. He continued. "Also, I will ask every doctor to do the same. After you make the list, I plan to call each one and tell them to mark off your charges."

He smiled. We stared—a freeway length stare. We were mute. Then at last, Jerry spoke: "Dr. Yu, I can't ask you to do that."

"No, you can't. And if you did, I would not do it." He laughed loudly.

We did not know what to say or do. Jerry looked at me and I at him. A cool and pleasant astonishment wrapped his face. "Why, Dr. Yu? Why are you doing this?"

He hesitated not at all, as he answered. "Because you are a man of God, and because it is right."

I gave Dr. Yu the information he had requested, and within a few days, he returned with the story, blazing with goodwill and intensity as he spoke. He met with both the CFO and the CEO of St. John's and had boldly laid out his proposal. They were astonished. They were contrary. They reminded Dr. Yu that the amount he was asking was nearly one-third of their annual charitable giving.

"So?" Dr. Yu said. "Gerald Buxton is a man of God, and this is right."

"You feel strongly about this, don't you George?"

"Yes, I do."

Conclusion? They would do it! Any money gained through litigation or from other petitions would go toward our account. The remaining debt would be wiped off the books.

He called the doctors, and with few exceptions, they too would write off our bills. (In total, we paid perhaps $5000.00 from our personal resources.)

The need for a miracle had come as a bolt that fateful Saturday afternoon in August. Since that time the word MIRACLE had continually nudged at us. It had lifted its dazzling head as death danced in the shadow and showed its pith to a mutilated body so nearly taken. Now on this grand afternoon, I realized that the astounding story Dr. Yu had just told us was not in the true sense the recounting of a miracle. Rather, it was a tale of human goodwill and of kindness.

Yet, in a pragmatic sense, I felt I sat in the presence of a miracle, of a supernatural happening. Had not we prayed and asked for the thing, although we had not asked in this way, for how could we have suspected such solution to a seemingly unsolvable problem? I had done all I could to gather money for this debt. Humanly, I had done all I could; yet it would not be enough and could not effect a resolution. Knowing that, I had done the only other thing I knew to do: I had asked for a miracle. To be honest, though, I am not sure I pled for a miracle. I did ask that God would help us and make provisions, but a miracle? Did I ask for that? Perhaps not, but that is what we got. Yes, it was a miracle, wrought by God and by Dr. Yu. I rose and embraced him.

The other remarkable development was associated with birds. An unusual tension had developed during the group therapy session on Friday, a day so warm that the windows were open. Rachel (not her actual name) was a beautiful young girl who several weeks before had undergone brain surgery to remove a malignant tumor. She had been doing well, but on her way into the group therapy room her doctor had stopped in the hall to tell her that the tumor was growing back. She was devastated, as was her family with her. During much of the therapy time, she and other patients had castigated the bedside manner of doctors and nurses. It was "bash doctors and nurses day," and it had gone on a long while. Dr. Jaffey listened and made pertinent remarks. Then she turned to Jerry as though for support. "Rev. Buxton, you have been quiet today. What do you think?"

Jerry agreed that Rachel's doctor had chosen a poor way to tell her this dreadful news, but he could not agree with those who were unhappy with the nursing care and with their doctors. "They have been wonderful to me here," he said. He continued, a message directed to every person in the room. "Some day this will seem only as a dream. We have suffered disappointments and setbacks in our lives, but we will not stay this way. These last weeks have been frightening ones for many of us. However, one day we will feel better. Our perspective will change, and we will see things differently."

He looked at his friends, a room full of them. Some were strapped into wheelchairs, as was he, others sat on straight chairs, having made their way down the hall using walkers or being helped with a cane. Tony wore a halo, and his chair lay back as he was not able to sit erect. Accident had selected them, or their bodies had failed them. He looked around the room, and reminded them, as he reminded himself: "Someday, the sun will shine as it has before. I am sure of it. The sun once more will shine, and the birds will sing again."

As though on a signal, very clearly and loudly, birds began to sing. Everyone heard them. I was there, and I heard them. Where moments before the room had been silent and tense, now trills filled the room. "My God," Tony exclaimed. "The man is a prophet. He said the birds would sing, and now they are singing!"

Dr. Jaffey brushed her arms and spoke of goose bumps. The tension left, and the session ended with smiles and positive words.

Who is to know the meaning of such thing? Was it supernatural, and if so, what was its significance? Why did the birds sing? Of only one thing am I absolutely sure: the birds *did* sing. On a still, warm afternoon with windows wide open, where birds had not sung, they at once commenced. If Heaven sent them, the angelic gifts were well received, for their presence silenced the moaning, and the spirit of the stricken was lifted.

Throughout this time, we spoke frequently and at length with the medical staff, planning Jerry's discharge. He would have several months of thrice weekly outpatient rehab, and we would stay in Dr. Yu's beach house while we were in Oxnard, spending the rest of the week in Rialto. Jerry had his J-tube removed, and now he ate all his food by mouth. Deliverymen brought in his new equipment, and we stood around and admired it. Andrew and Shauna gave up their rental home and moved into our place so that they could be ready to help with Jerry's care; the house was prepared for his wheelchair. I shopped for fine candy and took boxes to the emergency room, to the ICU, and to a couple of other places. A box of candy, though large and delicious, would not be good enough for rehab, so I ordered a gift basket of gigantic proportions and had it stuffed with the finest food and drink and delivered to the nurses' station.

The staff had planned a Christmas party for weeks, and Dr. Jaffey had asked Jerry to speak. They shoved all the equipment to the edge of the physical therapy room to make way for the celebration, and guests and patients formed a large circle that went around the walls. Some of our family were there, as were other friends and colleagues. There were gifts for the patients and the usual food and holiday activities that make up such a party. Dr. Jaffey played the piano and sang a Christmas song, then it was Jerry's turn, and someone rolled his chair so that all could see him. His Bible was in his lap. In his opening remarks, he spoke of his appreciation for St. John's and especially for the rehab unit. He thanked them for their superb efforts, efforts that had brought him from a level of near extinction, to one of progress and of extended hope. He gave credit to the medical staff—to doctors, nurses, and therapists—and he gave credit to God. With great effort, he opened his Bible to the second chapter of Luke that he had previously marked, and he began reading the magnificent Christmas story. It is the account of incarnation, of long ago night when God became a man. Shepherds had told it, as had angelic multitude. Now, in Oxnard, it was Jerry's turn. "And it came to pass in those days that there went out a decree from Caesar Augustus that all the world should be taxed." He read through the introductory verses, the middle ones, and to the significant conclusion. "And she brought forth her first born son, and wrapped him in swaddling clothes and laid Him in a manger because there was no room in the inn." The room cracked with emotion. Then Jerry was finished, and someone pushed him back to his place.

December 23 was the day of his discharge, and it was one of stirring excitement. *The Los Angeles Times* had come for a follow-up interview, and we spoke with the doctors. We made our rounds to say good-bye. We gathered things and hoped to leave nothing. The nurses gave me hospital gowns and draw sheets to turn Jerry in bed. We searched for Sam's cup but could not find it. Then it was time to leave.

The nurses and therapists bent over Jerry's chair, and with feeble arms, he held them. We cried. We gathered more things. We placed them in the car, and there, too, we placed him. We drove through the streets of Oxnard, then onto Highway 101. We headed south…toward home.

Healing

As rude and abrupt invader come disease and wound. Come as enemy, do they, insidious and stealthy or bold with furious slash of rabid frenzy. They advance to all and none escapes.

Although intermediary forces may reach into play, and more than one associate may be involved, all healing ultimately springs from singular source; that source is God. Apart from Him, there can be no healing, neither of the body nor of the invisible part of man, which is comprised of mind, soul, and spirit. It lies beyond the human scope to cure himself, yet it does appear that certain fevered ones have drawn healing unto themselves. By their pluck, or perhaps by chance or because of a particular discernment, they destine themselves for healing.

It seems timely to take a cursory look at four aspects of healing: homeostatic, medical, emotional, and spiritual. Although we will deal with the spiritual last, it is at once first, and of a certainty, we will detect its tendrils within each of the others.

Homeostasis, our natural healing system, is one of dynamic properties, but unfortunately, one to which we often pay scant attention. The tremendous machine called the human body has a few simple requirements: Adequate hours of rest and sleep, nutritious food in balanced amounts, and physical exercise. Although we will resolutely defend personal freedoms, surely we must reckon with extensive and widely accepted studies that have found recreational drugs to affect the human body in a negative way. This includes nicotine in all forms and alcoholic beverages. In addition, although admittedly one can do nothing about it, it bodes well to have selected forebears who lived long and healthy lives, as genetics seem to predispose one to certain sickness, or conversely, to days of abundant health.

Jerry scored well in his duel with accident; he does not smoke or drink, and although he had not strictly exercised, he was not sedentary but had been quite active. He had eaten balanced meals, and he slept long and well at night. As it became evident that he could live, the doctors said that his excellent living habits undoubtedly contributed to his recovery. Jerry's family stock is one of strength and longevity. His brother Herb is now in his mid-eighties, and his brother Jack reached his eighty-ninth year before dying.

Sometimes, healing must come in the form of medicines and of institutional care. In his view and in mine, Jerry received excellent medical care. There is no perfection, either in institutions or in persons, but we felt fortunate that Jerry had been treated at St. John's. The capable medical staff attended to his acute immediate needs and to his long-term medical care. The ambulance had been quick and efficient. Although all healing comes from God, He had used the hands of skilled doctors and nurses, and had directed their surgical techniques. Their minds had assessed his systemic needs, and from their stores they had drawn up and prescribed remedy for him. The therapists had been effective, transforming a helpless body into one of function and of purpose.

Invisible though they are, emotions play powerfully in the ebb and flow of life, and they influence greatly our response to daily challenges. Holy Scripture speaks to this in Proverbs 23:7: "For as he thinketh in his heart, so is he." Proverbs 17:22 records profoundly: "A merry heart doeth good like a medicine." Scientific studies in recent years have documented cases where positive emotional response seems connected to spontaneous and unusual healing. Conversely, those of negative mindset often fall into hopeless abyss where they quickly languish and die.

Many years ago, I read the absorbing account of Norman Cousins who, diagnosed with a specific disease, checked into a hotel and set about to cure himself by using laughter as therapy. Although he followed a certain amount of medical protocol, he attributed his recovery to laughter and to positive and uplifting thoughts. A few minutes of laughter, he said, would give him several hours of painless sleep.

We directed every positive emotional factor that we could imagine toward Jerry as he worked toward his healing. In Room 17, we played audiotapes of beautiful inspiring music. Steve read heartening verses of scripture aloud. We laughed. We touched him and kissed him. We told him he would be well again. We spoke of miracles. Finally, Jerry could join in the speaking and the doing, and his emotions sailed skyward. He told funny stories. He believed in himself and in his own recovery. He saw himself standing behind his familiar pulpit, where once more he would deliver the Word of God.

The human is a spiritual being, and although he exists in flesh and inhabits a body that God Himself created, his true self is one of spirit, eternal and intangible. We judge this so, lest at death our end should be thought to favor that of common beast, having no eternal substance or hope. Thus, the spiritual aspect of healing is truly relevant and one we cannot ignore.

Scripture is replete with accounts of the sick who came to Jesus, and of His healing them. Right there, instantaneously. He healed blind people that way, and crippled ones. The book of Luke records that once in the village of Nain as Jesus headed elsewhere, He encountered a funeral procession, and evidently decided that they should go no longer toward the graveyard. He just tore the whole thing up. I love to think of that. He hijacked that orderly sad funeral procession; he turned it around and changed it into something else—a festival! The dead was the only son of a grieving mother who plodded along beside his dead body. The heart of Jesus went out to the mother, and immediately He changed direction. He stepped right into the middle of the crowd and pushed aside the mourners. He told the mother not to cry, then placing his hand on the coffin, He spoke to the young man: "Get up." The boy heaved with new breath and popped up in his casket. The wailers stopped their wailing, and the mama quit her grieving. Jesus handed the boy to his mother and continued on His way.

Ill-considered it would be to suggest that supernatural spiritual healing is not a viable and germane part of twenty-first century life. Admittedly, healing is not wholly understood, nor does it seem to be at the absolute disposal of any certain individual or group. For could we at any moment call forth a supernatural healing, would we not go to operating chambers and heal them all? Yet, I make the call for such healing opportunity to be widely discussed. I plead for its being actively extended to all that have such need. Recent years have seen a resurgent interest in things of the Spirit and a craving for that of the supernatural. Well should this be understood, for our very natures are those of Spirit beings and of God-followers. Let no one disparage or scorn these inclinations.

Beginning at the first moment as I knelt alone with Jerry on Oxnard Blvd, until this very hour many months later, a miraculous spiritual healing has been that for which we prayed. Without that supernatural healing, Jerry would no doubt be dead today or bound still to his wheelchair, the quadriplegic banner waving fiercely above his head. Instead, the Master Healer's way met ours; His heart was moved, and He had compassion. Placing His hand on Jerry's body, He spoke with force and with authority: "Son, I say to you, Arise!"

The Return

"I came through and I shall return."
General Douglas MacArthur

27

The adjustment was monumental when Jerry came home. Our daily activities were as clothes we had once put off, and now as we donned them anew, their fit had changed. They smarted and chafed, some places hanging limply, others tight and restrictive. However, we adapted well, and our lives flowed smoothly. It took a very long time to do anything. I allowed two hours to get ready the first time we went to church together, and yet we were a few minutes late. Andrew and Shauna were a tremendous aid, and I do not know how we could have managed without them. They not only helped from the physical aspect, as with the lifting and such, but Andrew, especially, was of great spiritual inspiration and encouragement. In the early hours each morning, we heard him praying in his room. It gave us strength of measureless degree.

Brent Watts was a young minister who came with his wife and family to oversee the church until Jerry was able to do so. They were tremendous people, a joy to work with, and they served our church well.

Jerry spent several weeks in outpatient rehabilitation therapy, and he continued with his extraordinary recovery. From the use of the walker, he advanced to Canadian crutches, (those that clamp around the arm), and then to a cane. Only when we went out for long periods did he sit in his wheelchair. The therapists compiled a list of exercises Jerry should do at home, and then it was his last day. They discharged him.

A short, hinged brace that covered the distance just above to just below his knee had replaced the long leg brace on his left leg. He never took a step without it. He strapped it on each morning as he sat on the edge of the bed, and he took it off there in the evening. A craftsman had removed the door from our shower, and when Jerry was ready to bathe, he would sit on the shower chair and then remove the brace. When he was finished, he would replace it before taking even one step. His leg was completely unstable, and his orthopedic surgeon had said he must eventually have a total knee replacement.

We had been home several months when I walked into our bedroom and saw Jerry's leg brace laying on the bed. I was startled, not knowing what to make of this. In a moment, Jerry came walking into the room. "Your brace!" I think I half yelled at him. "Your brace is on the bed."

He appeared befuddled, and he sat down quickly and strapped on the brace. It took us a few minutes to ascertain what had transpired. He had noticed rain to be falling, and he wondered if the car windows were down, so he went to check. He had failed to put on his brace. How could he have forgotten that? We gazed at each other. Jerry sat on the edge of the bed with his hand on the brace, and I stood over him. Finally, after a few minutes we understood. Either one of two things had happened: the ligaments had grown again and reattached themselves, which doctors said could not happen, or in some miraculous way, he could walk despite not having those ligaments. He removed the brace and never wore it again!

It was September of 1995. Brent Watts left, and Jerry resumed the full charge of the church. Although it was difficult for him to admit, it proved to be extremely difficult for him to fulfill the duties of a pastor. He had always been a "hands-on" type minister who enjoyed being involved in all aspects of the church, and he could no longer physically do that. Pastoring is a highly charged emotional job, one that is filled with tension daily, and that calls for critical and quick decisions. It overwhelmed him, and he began to suspect that he probably should resign from his church in Rialto. He was at a crucial crossroads in his life, and it was truly a painful week as he struggled with the decision. They were wretched days. Steve and Andrew, our sons who are also ministers, stood with him as he struggled, as did I. Then he made up his mind: he would retire. We would leave Rialto.

He walked to the pulpit and read his resignation letter, concluding with Paul's wonderful remarks in II Corinthians 13:11: "Finally, brethren, farewell. Be perfect, be of good comfort, be of one mind."

It was the late fall of 1996, and Larry Booker became the new pastor. We leased out our house, had a gigantic garage sale, and put our furniture in storage. It was a bittersweet time, and although we did little of it before each other, I believe we both cried a lot. We already owned a large motor home, and we would travel extensively, something both of us enjoyed. The church body had been wonderful to us, and although we certainly were not wealthy, we should be comfortable, and we would be able to enjoy retirement years. Yet, there was a certain sadness to our days, and in some ways, we felt we were failures. Such mind-set was foreign to us and was a new way of thinking. Jerry spoke frankly of the dear people who made up the church and of their needs. "They deserve more than I can give them," he said to me once. We talked about perspective and of our advancing years and of new doors and opportunities. Several years earlier, Jerry and some of his friends had talked in favor of relatively early retirement, and had planned to travel together. They would not quit preaching altogether, but someone younger could take over their churches, giving them freedom they had never had. Yet, when Jerry's moment came, when virtually he *must* leave, he felt a scalding grief.

Another astonishing development was that Jerry was now able to drive our large motor home. He drove it to the church that last morning, and after the concluding service, we said our final goodbyes. We climbed into our vehicle and prepared to leave. We had mixed feelings, happiness shot through with sadness, and I recall thinking as we pulled near the edge of the parking lot: "I am not a pastor's wife anymore. Jerry is not a pastor." However, I saw new portals of intrigue and opportunity, and as I looked at Jerry as he pulled into the street, I saw that new vision had engulfed him.

Life beats us all. Mysterious and vaporous in creation, a new being spurts forth, its plump flesh rosy, gushing with Adam's juice. The quick intake of breath and the sharp wail are but the front edge of a grim continuum. Invisible yet, the deadly claws have revealed their tooth, for insidious and relentless, they work their scheme of death and decay. For now, though, Jerry and I had escaped. Just ahead of the whirlwind, we had danced a frantic cotillion, swinging always toward the passage of life and avoiding that of death and its greed.

That it was done with grace, let it be said.

Epilogue

Although taking a radical turn, Jerry's ministry has continued. He is in wide demand as a speaker and—should he choose to accept them—he has enough invitations to keep him engaged every week of the year. The focus of his preaching has changed drastically, and he often gives the testimony of his miraculous recovery when he speaks. It has engendered faith wherever he goes. He also speaks to ministerial groups and lectures at marriage seminars and in other retreat settings.

His body continues to improve. His wheelchair and walker are in storage along with the rest of our things. I think we gave away the Canadian crutches, and there may be a cane or two hanging about somewhere. He uses none of them. He has no pain, nor have his injuries caused him to need medication.

The months that have passed have given us time to think of what happened to us and to try to make sense of it. Flung into flaming crucible of adversity and woe, we learned anew to value our family and friends and to lean on Jesus. We had screamed a silent scream and Someone heard. A tornado had shattered us into a thousand pieces, but the Master came. We **did** survive.

Afterword

There are two things about this book that I would prefer to be different. The first is that I should have written more about Jerry's intimate feelings and about his close thoughts than I did. A more intense look into the working of his mind and possibly into his soul, if that were possible, would have been desirable. For him to have analyzed his deep thoughts concerning his paralysis would be of distinct interest, I believe. Fascinating reading could be crafted had he shared his contemplation of Frank, and his thoughts concerning the social mores of driving while drunk, for instance. I could not be dishonest and designate my own thoughts and conclusions as coming from Jerry's mouth, or from his thought processes. I was careful of such things, and when I attributed words or thoughts to him, one can know they were truly his.

Because of the dearth of such insights, I found myself writing more extensively of my own thoughts and feelings than I had planned. While I consider them to be of some interest, they certainly are secondary to any such information that would have come from Jerry himself.

The second shortcoming of the book? A few pages written personally by Jerry would form a tremendous addition. He chose otherwise, and I bow deeply to his wishes.

Medical Perspective

By

George Yu, MD, FACP, FCCP

I was in St. John's Regional Medical Center the day that Gerald
Buxton was taken there. I was called to the emergency room stat
to see this multiple trauma victim. He was intubated and on a
mechanical ventilator to assist his breathing. He had been hit by a car
and thrown 86 feet. There were fractures of the pelvis, femur, fibula,
and patella. His urinary bladder was ruptured. He had bilateral
multiple rib fractures with hemothoraces (blood in the chest cavities)
and lung contusion. A chest tube was inserted into his right thorax.
He had low blood pressure and low red blood cell count suggesting
active bleeding.

An orthopedic surgeon, a general surgeon, an urologist and a
plastic surgeon had already examined him. He was on his way to
the operating room to repair some of his fractures and to stop his
bleeding. In the operating room, I placed a chest tube into the left
thorax to expand his lung and to evacuate blood from his chest cavity.

In a span of three hours six physicians and surgeons had seen
Gerald. He received eight units of blood within the first 45 minutes
of his arrival in the ER, along with IV fluids to try to sustain his blood
pressure. In short, Gerald Buxton had suffered severe trauma with
massive hemorrhage.

I exited the operating room to talk with his family while the
surgeons were working on Gerald. There were many people in the
waiting room. I had a discussion with his wife regarding the severity
of his injuries and the treatment plan. As a pulmonary and critical
care specialist, I am accustomed to seeing individuals with massive
injuries, and have noted their response to treatment. I was not
optimistic about Gerald's prognosis that night. Our primary goal was

to keep him alive for the next forty-eight hours. If we were successful, maybe he would survive. In the next few weeks, physicians from five more specialties would see Gerald. In total, eleven medical and surgical specialties were involved in his care.

The next day, we found that his kidney function had deteriorated significantly. The likely cause was that his massive injury had led to muscle breakdown creating blockage within his kidneys. We placed him on intravenous fluids and gradually his kidney function returned to normal.

In the meantime, we noticed his gaze was abnormal. Dr. Herman, a neurosurgeon, was asked to see him. In the ensuing few days, Gerald developed progressive arm and leg weakness. A CAT scan of the neck revealed fracture of the sixth and seventh cervical vertebrae (bones in the spine), the spinal cord was compressed and was causing his arms and legs weakness. In order to stabilize his spine and prevent further injury, Dr. Herman performed neck surgery and a metal halo was inserted to immobilize his head and neck. For the next few weeks, his head was held in a perpetual upright and neutral position.

We thought the worst of his medical problems was taken care of and turned our attention to his nutrition. We encouraged Gerald to eat a soft diet. Right away, he developed a fever, and his chest X-ray showed pneumonia in his right lung. We were concerned that some of the food had gone down to his lungs instead of to his stomach. I performed a fiberoptic bronchoscopy to examine his vocal cords, trachea and lungs. His cough was very weak and he was unable to bring up his secretions. In order to prevent further aspiration and worsening of his pneumonia, Gerald was placed back on the ventilator that took over most of the breathing for him.

Just when we thought his condition had stabilized, his abdomen became distended, followed by vomiting. An ultrasound examination of his abdomen showed an enlarged gallbladder. Dr. Cardan, a general surgeon, was called to see Gerald. Inflammation of the gallbladder was suspected and surgical exploration of his abdomen followed.

An inflamed gallbladder was found and removed. Afterwards, Gerald was placed on intravenous feeding through a vein under his collarbone. A low-grade fever persisted and infectious disease specialist Dr. Oster was consulted. A blood test for Candida (yeast) infection was positive. Appropriate antibiotic was begun.

Finally, Gerald was ready for the next phase of his recovery—the Rehabilitation Service. During this phase of his therapy, Gerald was under the care of Dr. Herbert Judy, a rehabilitation specialist. He would spend the next three months in the rehab facility on F Street.

At the time of admission to the rehabilitation service, Gerald was totally dependent on others to assist in his activities of daily living. When he left the hospital on December 23, he was able to sit up from a recumbent position and then stand up with minimal assistance. He was able to ambulate with a front wheel walker for 120 feet on level surfaces. In addition, he was able to propel himself in a wheelchair for 400 feet in 4 minutes. To say this was a remarkable recovery is an understatement.

In the next few years, Gerald would put away his walker and cane and walk without assistance. He would even play golf. Why did this man recover? Without invoking divine intervention, I submit that his will to live, unwavering religious faith, and the love of his family and friends were the keys to his survival and ultimate recovery. He lives to bear witness to the power of faith, hope, and love. On a number of occasions, I have talked with Gerald about his ordeal. I am struck by his absolute faith in God, and in his health care team. His religious calling may have convinced him there is unfinished work in his ministry. I have no doubt that his recovery is an inspiration to all of us who have the privilege of knowing him.

About the Author

Besides being the wife of Jerry and mother to their four children, Shirley Buxton is the grandmother to Chris, Joel, Sarah, Jessica, Kelly, Ryan, Nathaniel, Chloe, Gentry, and Cole. Evan is her great grandchild. Her family is the joy of her life.

She also is the president of the Ladies Ministries of the Western District of the United Pentecostal Church, International. The Western District is comprised of the states of California and Nevada. Each year, she plans and coordinates two large ladies conferences.

Although this is her first book, she has been a published writer for many years. For a lengthy period, she was a regular writer for Word Aflame Publications. She is a frequent contributor to monthly magazines.

She teams with her husband to minister at marriage retreats and other religious services. On her own, she often is a speaker at ladies functions.

What Readers are Saying

A Thousand Pieces! What a fitting title for an incredible book. Having known the Buxtons since before their marriage, it is a great privilege to recommend this book to you. As I carefully absorbed each paragraph, my emotions ran the gamut of feelings. However, three things came through with incredible impact.

First was **tragedy,** then **travail,** and finally **triumph.** The tragedy was of immense proportion, followed by the travail of family, friends, and church, and then finally there came the triumph. This book documents the faithfulness of God and the faithfulness of Jerry and Shirley.

A Thousand Pieces was put together by the only one who could.....our God! Read, enjoy, and allow your faith to grow.

Charles Grisham
Author, Conference Speaker
Pastor of New Life Apostolic Church
Detroit, Michigan

How could I not help but savor and devour every word, every thought and every emotion captured on the pages of this book? So clear is the description, that I found myself standing on the curb next to the abandoned Landcruiser, pacing in the waiting room as the family's hopes dangled from reality, and praising an incredible God who answers prayer from His vantage point and in His time. Shirley Buxton has allowed the reader to enter the private spaces of their lives and has permitted us to share in the ecstasy of their miracle. Don't even start this book unless you're ready to laugh and to cry, to question and to cheer, to moan and to thank our Lord Jesus Christ.

Edward Cantu
Pastor of Family Worship Center
Monument, Colorado

King David once said: "I had fainted, unless I had believed to see the goodness of the LORD in the land of the living." Psalm 27:13 In this inspirational book you will see that sometimes bad things happen to good Godly people. However, your faith will also be strengthened as you read how this tragedy was turned into a great victory. Tragedy was turned into a miracle because friends, family, and church banded together with prayer and faith. Jesus stretched forth his hand and delivered Gerald Buxton out of the "valley of the shadow of death."

This book will demonstrate, again, the truth of the passage in Romans 8:28. "For we know that all things work together for good to them that love God, to them who are the called according to His purpose."

In unusual ways, God reached out and touched people's lives with His power, grace, and gospel. Perhaps, otherwise, these people would have never been touched.

Larry Alred
Pastor of Life Tabernacle
Ventura, California

I have read thousands of books in my life. Some of them were truly memorable: they stood out from the ordinary because of some enduring quality or feature.

A Thousand Pieces is a book that will endure in my memory. It is a beautifully written true story that will repeatedly bring you to tears. Yet, it is not a sad story. No, it is so much more than that: it is a story of inspirational love, faith, and victory.

This is a story filled with desperate crises, battle after battle and victory after victory. This book is worth reading because it relates an amazing tale of horrific tragedy overcome through the grace of God. It is, also, worth reading because of the pure beauty and flow of its prose. Most of all, this book should be read for those chapters and passages where it seems that God must have guided the pen of the author as she wrote with anointing about pain, the will of God, spiritual growth, society, love and faith. These passages are literary masterpieces, spiritual insights, and holy revelations.

In this book, many will find the strength to look up with faith to Him whose grace is ever sufficient in any situation.

Donald H. O'Keefe
Author, Missionary
Pastor of United Pentecostal Church
Pittsburg, California

To reorder or to find out about
other great books by Forrest
Press please visit us at:

www.forrestpressusa.com

Forrest Press